WORLD HISTORY SERIES

The Computer Revolution

by
John M. Dunn

Lucent Books, 10911 Technology Place, San Diego, CA 92127

Library of Congress Cataloging-in-Publication Data

Dunn, John M., 1949–
    The computer revolution / John M. Dunn.
        p. cm. — (World history series)
Includes bibliographical references (p.) and index.
    ISBN 1-56006-848-5
    1. Computers—History. I. Title. II. Series.
    QA76.17 .D86 2002
    004'.09—dc21

                                        2001002557

Copyright 2002 by Lucent Books, Inc., 10911 Technology Place
San Diego, California 92127

Printed in the U.S.A.

Contents

Foreword

Each year on the first day of school, nearly every history teacher faces the task of explaining why his or her students should study history. One logical answer to this question is that exploring what happened in our past explains how the things we often take for granted—our customs, ideas, and institutions—came to be. As statesman and historian Winston Churchill put it, "Every nation or group of nations has its own tale to tell. Knowledge of the trials and struggles is necessary to all who would comprehend the problems, perils, challenges, and opportunities which confront us today." Thus, a study of history puts modern ideas and institutions in perspective. For example, though the founders of the United States were talented and creative thinkers, they clearly did not invent the concept of democracy. Instead, they adapted some democratic ideas that had originated in ancient Greece and with which the Romans, the British, and others had experimented. An exploration of these cultures, then, reveals their very real connection to us through institutions that continue to shape our daily lives.

Another reason often given for studying history is the idea that lessons exist in the past from which contemporary societies can benefit and learn. This idea, although controversial, has always been an intriguing one for historians. Those who agree that society can benefit from the past often quote philosopher George Santayana's famous statement, "Those who cannot remember the past are condemned to repeat it." Historians who subscribe to Santayana's philosophy believe that, for example, studying the events that led up to the major world wars or other significant historical events would allow society to chart a different and more favorable course in the future.

Just as difficult as convincing students of the importance of studying history is the search for useful and interesting supplementary materials that present historical events in a context that can be easily understood. The volumes in Lucent Books' World History Series attempt to present a broad, balanced, and penetrating view of the march of history. Ancient Egypt's important wars and rulers, for example, are presented against the rich and colorful backdrop of Egyptian religious, social, and cultural developments. The series engages the reader by enhancing historical events with these cultural contexts. For example, in *Ancient Greece*, the text covers the role of women in that society. Slavery is discussed in *The Roman Empire*, as well as how slaves earned their freedom. The numerous and varied aspects of everyday life in these and other societies are explored in each volume of the series. Additionally, the series covers the major political, cultural, and philosophical ideas as the torch of civilization is passed from ancient Mesopotamia and Egypt, through Greece, Rome, Medieval Europe, and other world cultures, to the modern day.

The material in the series is formatted in a thorough, precise, and organized manner. Each volume offers the reader a comprehensive and clearly written overview of an important historical event or period. The topic under discussion is placed in a broad, historical context. For example, *The Italian Renaissance* begins with a discussion of the High Middle Ages and the loss of central control that allowed certain Italian cities to develop artistically. The book ends by looking forward to the Reformation and interpreting the societal changes that grew out of the Renaissance. Thus, students are not only involved in a historical era, but also enveloped by the events leading up to that era and the events following it.

One important and unique feature in the World History Series is the primary and secondary source quotations that richly supplement each volume. These quotes are useful in a number of ways. First, they allow students access to sources they would not normally be exposed to because of the difficulty and obscurity of the original source. The quotations range from interesting anecdotes to farsighted cultural perspectives and are drawn from historical witnesses both past and present. Second, the quotes demonstrate how and where historians themselves derive their information on the past as they strive to reach a consensus on historical events. Lastly, all of the quotes are footnoted, familiarizing students with the citation process and allowing them to verify quotes and/or look up the original source if the quote piques their interest.

Finally, the books in the World History Series provide a detailed launching point for further research. Each book contains a bibliography specifically geared toward student research. A second, annotated bibliography introduces students to all the sources the author consulted when compiling the book. A chronology of important dates gives students an overview, at a glance, of the topic covered. Where applicable, a glossary of terms is included.

In short, the series is designed not only to acquaint readers with the basics of history, but also to make them aware that their lives are a part of an ongoing human saga. Perhaps then they will come to the same realization as famed historian Arnold Toynbee. In his monumental work, *A Study of History*, he wrote about becoming aware of history flowing through him in a mighty current, and of his own life "welling like a wave in the flow of this vast tide."

IMPORTANT DATES IN THE COMPUTER REVOLUTION

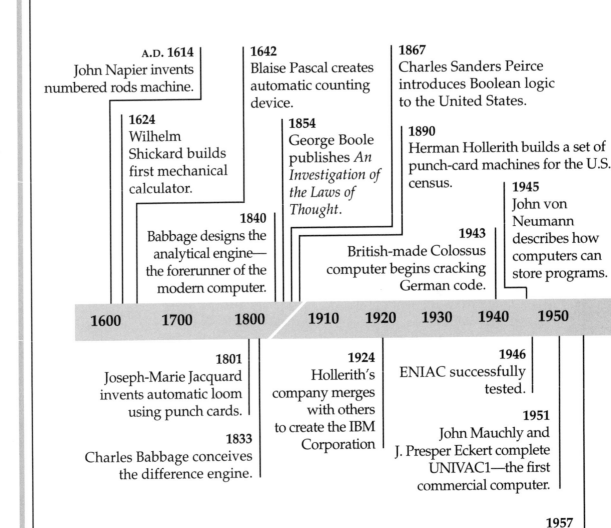

A.D. 1614
John Napier invents numbered rods machine.

1624
Wilhelm Shickard builds first mechanical calculator.

1642
Blaise Pascal creates automatic counting device.

1854
George Boole publishes *An Investigation of the Laws of Thought*.

1840
Babbage designs the analytical engine—the forerunner of the modern computer.

1867
Charles Sanders Peirce introduces Boolean logic to the United States.

1890
Herman Hollerith builds a set of punch-card machines for the U.S. census.

1943
British-made Colossus computer begins cracking German code.

1945
John von Neumann describes how computers can store programs.

1600   1700   1800   1910   1920   1930   1940   1950

1801
Joseph-Marie Jacquard invents automatic loom using punch cards.

1833
Charles Babbage conceives the difference engine.

1924
Hollerith's company merges with others to create the IBM Corporation

1946
ENIAC successfully tested.

1951
John Mauchly and J. Presper Eckert complete UNIVAC1—the first commercial computer.

1957
Seymor Cray and William Norris found Control Data Company.

1977
ARPA successfully tests TCP by connecting ARPAnet with ALOHAnet and SATnet; the birth of the Internet; Apple II computer makes its debut; Bill Gates and Paul Allen write BASIC program for Altair Computer.

1964
Cray's CDC 6600 becomes fastest computer.

1979
USEnet founded and followed by other computer networks.

1975
Altair PC kit goes on sale.

1980s
Use of PCs becomes widespread.

1974
Intel announces 8008 microchip.

1989
Eighty thousand host computers connected to Internet; ARPAnet taken off-line; Tim Berners-Lee creates World Wide Web software.

1973
Vinton Cerf and Robert Kahn create Transmission Control Protocol (TCP).

1991
CERN makes Web software free to the world.

1992
U.S. Congress legalizes commercial activity on the Internet.

1960	1965	1970	1975	1980	1985	1990	1995	2000

1976
Steve Jobs and Steve Wozniak build Apple I computer.

1985
Microsoft responds with its GUI-based Windows system.

1996
100 million users on the Internet.

1960
Paul Baran conceives new communication network for ARPA.

1981
IBM joins PC market.

1984
Apple announces Macintosh with GUI.

1958
Bell Labs announces first transistor.

1980
Gates and Allen found Microsoft Corporation; Apple is PC industry leader.

1983
ARPAnet splits. One part connects with other networks; the other becomes MILnet for military purposes.

A Quiet Revolution

Revolutions are the impetus for turning points in history. They are the huge events that dramatically transform human life. These upheavals are powerful enough to shake empires to pieces and give birth to new ones. In a revolution, old beliefs, values, customs, and patterns of behaviors disappear as new social patterns unfold.

Some revolutions are violent and bloody. Many are imposed by external warring enemies; others are motivated by greed, religious fervor, or dreams of conquest. Yet others arise from within, triggered by perceptions of injustice, inequality, and cruelty. Calamity is another parent of revolution. Volcanic explosions, earthquakes, droughts, and pestilence all have razed past civilizations and paved the way for their replacements.

Invention, discovery, and exploration, also have shaken human societies. Johannes Gutenberg's creation of the movable-type printing press more than five centuries ago, the discovery that the center of the solar system is the sun, not the earth, plus the prowling of unfamiliar seas by Spanish and Portuguese ships gave rise to a series of transformations: the Renaissance, the Scientific Revolution, the Enlightenment, and the Industrial Revolution—changes of epic proportions that still affect the nations of the world.

By the end of the twentieth century, a new kind of revolution was underway. It was typified by the gentle tapping of human fingers against electronic keyboards, and the soft clicking of an electronic device called a mouse. Hundreds of millions of pairs of human eyes stared into electronic boxes filled with flashing light, scrolling words, and various sounds.

Those activities continue today, as increasing numbers of individuals around the world join the Computer Revolution. As they command their machines to do their bidding, the economic, political, and social structures upon which their lives are based are giving way to new arrangements.

At the heart of this quiet revolution is the modern personal computer. The product of centuries of human thought and tinkering, this astounding new machine is steadily transforming the world. Now, at the dawn of the twenty-first century, computers are everywhere. Homes, schools, churches, marketplaces, factories, governments, military establishments, cars, planes, trains—all are equipped with computers. So, too, are growing numbers of people who carry computers in their briefcases and even in their pockets.

Like no other machine, the computer has boosted human power to immeasurable levels. Using one of these devices, an individual can do the work of hundreds of workers a century ago. With a few keystrokes, a single person can execute commands and remotely control machinery at the edges of the solar system, the bottom of the sea, or, one day soon, inside the blood vessel of a human being.

Spawned by the computer is another marvel—the Internet. An ever-unfurling global web of wires, cables, and radio and microwave transmissions devices, this vast communication system connects hundreds of millions of computers and their users. This international system facilitates communication on a scale never before imagined. Globally, people can e-mail images and messages, and even speak to and see each other. They can transmit electronic versions of financial fortunes or the contents of entire libraries from one side of the world to the next without ever needing a single postage stamp.

Portable personal computers such as laptops allow people to work, communicate with others, and access information from nearly anywhere.

Patrons at a cyber cafe use the Internet, a system that links computers and puts huge amounts of information at the user's fingertips.

Vast resources of information are now available to anyone with a personal computer and the necessary gear to connect to the Internet. Increasing numbers of universities, libraries, businesses, research centers, public institutions, governments, and private groups and individuals of all types post websites on the Internet for all the world to share.

This vast interconnectivity of human thought on a global basis is unique in history. It has the power to embolden the individual, while at the same time creating new borderless communities. However, this technology may also be creating a universe of isolated and transfixed individuals who are responding to the disembodied words and ideas of strangers, rather than communicating in person with their neighbors.

This trend toward isolation is just one aspect of the dark side of the Computer Revolution. Other problems exist, too. Hate mongers, criminals, terrorists, the deviant,

and the perverted also have access to new personal power offered by the computer. In their hands, the computer and the Internet could become tools of global menace.

The Computer Revolution is also accelerating change. Newer and ever-faster machines both empower and overwhelm human societies. "New computer chips are immediately put to use developing the next generation of more powerful ones. . . . Technologies with this property of self-accelerated development . . . create conditions that are unstable, unpredictable, and unreliable," warns author Stewart Brand.[1]

Because computers are still so new, nobody yet fully understands their impact on the physical, mental, and spiritual lives of humans. Exhilarating, frustrating, baffling, and even sometimes terrifying, the Computer Revolution is now a permanent feature of modern life. However, its full story is yet to be played out. This revolution is still only in its infancy.

1 Origins of the Revolution

Though the modern computer is a product of the twentieth century, the history of its predecessors is ancient. The story begins thousands of years ago, when early humans first learned to count in order to keep track of their possessions, transactions, and the passage of time. Most likely, primitive people used their own toes and fingers to count. A reminder of this prehistoric practice is found today in the word digit, which means any number zero to nine. The word's origin, however, is the Latin *digitus,* meaning finger.

As ancient societies became more complex, people developed tools for counting. Ancient Sumerians, for example, made scratch marks on pieces of sun-baked clay, while the Incas of Peru tied knots in pieces of rope. Early Europeans counted their livestock by matching each animal with a stone. This is why another Latin word—*calculus,* meaning stone—became the root of the modern word calculate.

All these early tools seemed clumsy and antiquated before the arrival of the abacus— the first true personal calculating device. First appearing in Asia more than five thousand years ago, this device later spread into Europe and the Arabic-speaking lands. A typical abacus consisted of a wood frame that housed rows of thin parallel rods or wires. Operators of the apparatus used colored beads or other circular objects as counters and slid them into various positions along the rods. Each row represented a different mathematical value. A bead on the first row, for example, might have had a value of one; the second was worth ten, and so on.

Reliable and simple to use, the abacus satisfied most human calculating requirements for centuries. Even advanced nations such as Russia used them well into the twentieth century. But the abacus had its limits. It was not as efficient as another kind of machine that many humans had long dreamed of: one that could calculate automatically.

The abacus, an early calculator, used beads strung on rods as counters.

THE SEARCH FOR MECHANICAL COMPUTERS

Among the first people to conceive a mechanical calculator was the Renaissance painter and inventor Leonardo da Vinci (1452–1519), who designed a machine with thirteen decimal wheels and devices for carrying numbers to the next column. All that is known about Leonardo's machine are his design plans. Nobody knows for certain if he, or anyone else, ever built the device.

In 1614, Scottish politician, magician, and military weapons designer John Napier went a step further than Leonardo. Napier actually built an apparatus that enabled its users to multiply and divide large numbers without having to use pen and paper. Instead, work was done on specially numbered rods (nicknamed "Napier's bones"). When correctly arranged side by side, the rods indicated sums and products of various math problems. Eventually Napier's bones provided the basis for another early mechanical calculator—the slide rule, a handheld device with sliding numbered scales that was still being used in universities until personal computers made them obsolete in the 1970s.

Napier was not alone in the search to build a calculating machine. In 1624, German inventor Wilhelm Shickard crafted what some scholars consider to be the world's first mechanical calculator. Based on Napier's principles, Shickard's machine relied on rotating cylinders instead of rods. Eleven complete and six incomplete sprockets enabled operators of the calculator to add numbers. With the help of special logarithm tables, the machine could also multiply and divide. Initially Shickard built his machine to help cal-

culate the movement of astronomical bodies. All traces of his creation, however, disappeared during the Thirty Years' War (1618–1648) in Europe. For centuries afterward, few knew of his invention. Then in 1957 a letter written by Shickard to the German astronomer Johannes Kepler surfaced and rekindled interest in the pioneering calculator.

In 1642 another mechanical calculator appeared. It was built by nineteen-year-old French scientist and philosopher Blaise Pascal, who called his creation the Pascaline. Weary from adding long columns of figures in his father's accounting office, Pascal put together a shoe-box-sized machine that allowed its operator to automatically add numbers by turning a series of interlocking wheels, cogs, and numbered dials. Pascal once proudly described his invention this way: "I submit to the public a small machine by my invention, by means of which you alone may, without any effort, perform all the operations of arithmetic, and may be relieved of the work which has often times fatigued your spirit."[2]

During the next few years, other calculating machines appeared that were capable of carrying out more varieties of mathematical operations than the Pascaline. English inventor Sir Samuel Morland, for example, crafted a device that allowed users to multiply and divide. And in 1673 a young German professor, Gottfried Wilhelm Leibniz, exhibited his Stepped Reckoner at the Royal Society in London. Considered an improvement on the Pascaline, Leibniz's machine required the use of a hand crank, plus a series of cylinders and gears that permitted the user to multiply, divide, and even determine square roots.

As clever as these devices were, they had serious drawbacks: They were unreliable and awkward to use, and all were single-purpose calculators incapable of being programmed with a set of instructions that enabled them to do a variety of mathematical functions.

A solution to the programming problem soon emerged in an area far removed from that of calculating machines. For many years silk manufacturers in France had sought ways to change weaving patterns without having to make major adjustments to their looms. In 1801 weaver Joseph-Marie Jacquard developed an automated textile loom that controlled the warp and weft of threads on a silk loom with an endless chain of cards with punched holes that matched a particular design. When the cards made contact with a row of needles, those needles that matched up with holes stayed in place while the others moved forward. The location of the needles determined the pattern to be woven. Jacquard's technique enabled weavers to automatically introduce new intricate patterns into their work by changing punched cards. Though praised by the French government for his innovation, Jacquard was eventually forced to flee the city of Lyon to avoid the wrath of French weavers who were enraged that the automatic loom eliminated many of their jobs.

Jacquard's use of punched cards as a way of programming a machine to perform a particular task caught the attention of Englishman Charles Babbage, a nineteenth-century economist and mathematician noted for his high intellect and cranky mannerisms. Babbage, also a founding member of the Royal Astronomical Society,

English economist and mathematician Charles Babbage devised a plan for his first calculating machine, the Difference engine, in 1833.

firmly believed his fellow English countrymen needed more accurate and up-to-date ways of calculating the many complex mathematical tasks needed by a young and growing industrial nation. At the time, the mathematical tables used by navigators, astronomers, and craftsmen, were riddled with errors. Those who tried to create their own tables were doomed to many long hours of complicated and repetitive computations.

Babbage wondered if a machine could be devised to free human beings from having to do these irksome tasks. In 1833, with financial backing from the British government, he conceived the Difference engine—a machine whose purpose was to create mathematical tables with computations derived by comparing the differences between various numbers. Babbage also intended his machine to do something else earlier machines could not do: print the results. The Difference engine, however, was never built. Engineering problems and an end of government funding forced the inventor to abandon the project after spending ten years developing it.

Undaunted, Babbage disclosed new plans in 1840 for another machine. This machine was even more elaborate than the Difference engine; Babbage called it the Analytical engine. It was unlike any other mechanical calculator ever imagined. Babbage's plans called for a room-sized, steam-powered, all-purpose machine that was capable of performing any number of calculating tasks, not just producing mathematical tables.

But the Analytical engine's design was also unique in other ways. In fact, it was so revolutionary that many historians consider it the mechanical precursor to the modern electronic computer. Like the computer of the twentieth century, the analytical engine was intended to have a "store," or memory, that saved results for later use. It would also house another device called a mill—a central processing unit similar to that of a modern computer—which could perform arithmetic calculations. Babbage had also designed an apparatus that could print the results of computations. Finally, the machine was designed to be programmable. Input, or information, could be introduced to the machine with punched cards, much like a French loom. "We may say most aptly that the Analytical Engine weaves *algebraical patterns* just as the Jacquard-loom weaves flowers and leaves,"

wrote admirer and assistant of Babbage, Ada Agusta, the Countess of Lovelace, daughter of famed poet Lord Byron.[3] Agusta was an accomplished mathematician who wrote various calculations that she hoped one day would provide a series of instructions, or programs, on punched cards for Babbage's yet unbuilt machine. These writings later earned her the title of history's first computer programmer.

Scott McCartney, author of *ENIAC: The Triumphs and Tragedies of the World's First Computer*, believes the analytical engine's most important design feature was that "[It] had a key function that distinguishes computers from calculators: the conditional statement."[4] This meant the machine's behavior depended on the computation that had last occurred; it was designed to perform in various ways, each depending on what event preceded it.

Once again, however, design problems proved insurmountable and Babbage never completed the machine. Only his plans, drawings, and a few engine parts survived after his death. Not until the end of the nineteenth century did the idea of a computer running on punched cards become a reality.

HOLLERITH'S MACHINE

The next big development took place in the United States. In 1890 the nation's government faced the daunting task of conducting a population census. Always a complicated job, this census was expected to be especially difficult. For the previous census, hundreds of federal workers had labored for seven and a half years to tabulate statistical information

An Unfinished Dream

Charles Babbage, creator of the analytical engine, ended his life as a sad old man. John Fletcher Moulton, a mathematician at Cambridge University in England, provides this eyewitness description of the inventor's final days in Stan Augarten's book Bit by Bit: An Illustrated History of Computers.

In the first room I saw the parts of the original Calculating Machine, which had been shown in an incomplete state many years before and had even been put to some use. I asked him about its present form. "I have not finished it because in working at it I came on the idea of my Analytical Engine, which would do all that it was capable of doing and much more. Indeed the idea was so much simpler that it would have taken more work to complete the calculating machine than to design and construct the other in its entirety, so I turned my attention to the Analytical Machine." After a few minutes' talk we went into the next workroom where he showed and explained to me the working of the elements of the Analytical Machine. I asked if I could see it. "I have never completed it," he said, "because I hit upon the idea of doing the same thing by a different and far more effective method, and this rendered it useless to proceed on the old lines." Then we went into the third room. There lay scattered bits of mechanism but I saw no trace of any working machine. Very cautiously I approached the subject, and received the dreaded answer, "It is not constructed yet, but I am working at it, and will take less time to construct it altogether than it would have taken to complete the Analytical Machine from the stage in which I left it." I took leave of the old man with a heavy heart.

on 50 million people. Since then, the nation's population had grown by an estimated 12 million, causing many census officials to fear they would be unable to finish the 1890 census before the next one arrived. So, they turned to Herman Hollerith, a young American engineer who designed a calculating machine specifically for the census.

To make use of the machine, workers first had to transfer population data that had been collected in written forms and encoded onto punch cards. Each card had twelve rows with twenty holes punched into different patterns. The location of each hole on the card represented information about a person's date of birth, gender, age, and other facts. Though these punch cards resembled those that Charles Babbage had in mind, Hollerith most likely did not get the idea from him. Instead, Hollerith was probably

American engineer Herman Hollerith created a calculating machine for the 1890 census.

inspired by railroad conductors of his day. To keep track of their passengers, the conductors punched holes in train tickets in certain patterns to indicate passengers' physical characteristics such as sex, race, and hair color.

When the punch cards were rolled onto Hollerith's machines, they made contact with 288 spring-loaded pins that poked against them. Pins passed through any holes, made contact with cups of mercury, and completed electrical circuits. The resulting flow of electricity caused various dials on the machine to register the results. In this way, the government could assemble data in various ways. For example, census workers could, if they chose, count the number of immigrant women from Italy over the age

of thirty who had three children. This ability to use a machine to sort facts in multiple combinations was revolutionary. As Scott McCartney points out, "For the first time, electricity and computing were converging as intelligence inside a machine. It made for a smaller machine because it made for a faster machine."[5]

Hollerith's census machines were a success. In fact, they worked so well that the Census Bureau had completed its work in one-third of the time it had needed to complete the previous census. This accomplishment saved the government $5 million. Census officials were also pleased that Hollerith's machine tallies were more accurate than any others.

Buoyed by his success, Hollerith formed a business called the Tabulating Machine Company in 1896, and sold versions of his machine worldwide. By 1924 his company merged with others and acquired a new name: the International Business Machines Corporation, or IBM, a company that later became one of the world's leading manufacturers of modern computers.

AN UNDERLYING NUMBER SYSTEM

As Hollerith and other engineers worked to perfect mechanical computers, mathematicians were making progress in a different area that would one day pave the way for the modern computer: a powerful system of logic.

All computational devices, whether a simple abacus or a large, complex modern mainframe computer, require some type of underlying mathematical system upon which to operate. Almost all the early mechanical computers used the familiar ten-digit decimal system (zero through nine). Though adequate for everyday pen and paper calculations, this number system eventually proved inefficient in computers. For example, mechanical calculators and even electromechanical calculators (those developed by contemporaries of Hollerith that used a combination of electrical switches and machine parts) were generally large contraptions consisting of many complex working parts that required constant adjusting, oiling, and maintenance. Such systems became only more complicated and cumbersome when a number system based on ten was used for computations.

But a modern computer uses a number system based on two digits. This binary system proved to be simpler, more efficient, and easier to use when computers finally became fully electronic.

THE DREAM OF A BINARY SYSTEM

With a base that uses only two digits—0 and 1—the binary system represents a way of thinking that has fascinated philosophers, mathematicians, and engineers for centuries, though none of them could have ever guessed it would one day serve as the primary mathematical basis for modern computers.

Many past thinkers, especially intellectuals who specialized in logic and philosophy, admired the simplicity of the binary system. It uses just two propositions to establish the truth or falsity of a statement. This often took the form of a yes or no, true or false, existence or nonexistence.

For the most part, however, the binary system remained an obscure academic topic understood by only a few until self-taught British mathematician George Boole began studying it during the nineteenth century at about the same time Babbage dwelled on his analytical engine. In his 1854 book *An Investigation of the Laws of Thought*, Boole proposed a new type of logic that was expressed in symbols used in algebra rather than everyday language. Until this time, the only other logic-based system to use symbols was geometry, developed by the Greek thinker Euclid a thousand years before. Boole's system offered a way to express the processes of human thought in mathematical terms. At the heart of his algebra were two states: the universe and nothing, that Boole designated with the signs of 1 and 0—terms still used in computer design today.

British mathematician George Boole based his Boolean logic on the binary system.

Howard Rheingold, author of *Tools for Thought: The History and Future of Mind Expanding Technology*, explains the significance of Boole's concept on future computers:

> When the different parts of computer technology converged unexpectedly a hundred years later, electrical engineers needed mathematical tools to make sense of the complicated machinery they were inventing. The networks of switches they created were electrical circuits whose behavior could be described and predicted by precise equations. Because patterns of electrical pulses were now used to encode logical operations like "and," "or," and the all-important "if," as well as the calculator's usual fare of "plus," "minus," "multiply," and "divide," there arose the need for equations to describe the logical properties of computer circuits. [6]

Boolean logic, as it came to be known, eventually served this purpose. But during Boole's lifetime, his new kind of algebra created enthusiasm among only a few mathematicians. One of them was Charles Sanders Pierce, an American logician, who published essays on Boolean logic in 1867 that introduced the new concepts to many American mathematicians, engineers, and scientists. Pierce continued his study of Boole's ideas for almost another twenty years. During that time, he made a profound discovery: Boolean algebra could revolutionize how electric switching circuits operated. Pierce realized that the same equations used to determine the truth and falsity of a proposition in logic could also be used to create on-and-off situations for the flow of electrons from one junction in a wiring circuit to the next. Despite his insight, he never built such circuits. That task he left to others.

COMPUTERS BECOME ELECTRONIC

The first researcher to take up the cause was Claude Shannon, a twenty-one-year-old graduate student at Massachusetts Institute

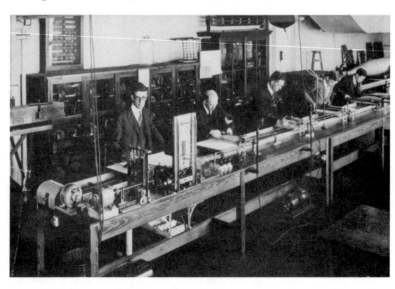

Vannevar Bush (left), a professor at MIT, and his assistants experiment with calculating machines. MIT student Claude Shannon believed that Bush's machine could be improved by using electricity.

Physicist and mathematician John V. Atanasoff pioneered the use of electronic vacuum tubes in computers.

of Technology (MIT). In 1936, Shannon accepted the challenge of trying to improve a mechanical computing device called the differential analyzer, built by Vannevar Bush, a professor at MIT. Though the machine could solve complex math problems, it was big and bulky and had many oily mechanical parts that often broke.

Shannon realized, as Pierce once had, the stunning possibilities of Boolean algebra. In 1938 Shannon published his master's thesis, entitled "A Mathematical Theory of Communication," in which he argued that information could be transmitted by electrical impulses controlled by on and off switches.

Others were also discovering the beauty of binary mathematics. One of them was John V. Atanasoff, a mathematician and physicist at Iowa State College, who decided to abandon the decimal system in favor of the binary system for an electromechanical computer he was building. His device also was the first to use electronic vacuum tubes—sealed electronic glass containers

with no working parts that controlled the on and off flow of electricity. The arrival of vacuum tubes signaled the beginning of electronic computers and the slow demise of exclusively mechanical computers.

Yet another American, George Stibitz, a research mathematician with Bell Labs, reached the conclusion that Boolean algebra could improve circuits used in telephone systems. He and a colleague, Samuel Williams, devised an electromechanical machine in 1939 that used Boolean logic to multiply and divide complex numbers, a function needed to perform telephone switching operations. Previously, a group of ten company employees had to make these calculations every day.

Meanwhile, engineer Konrad Zuse in Germany was also making similar breakthroughs. Unaware of Boolean algebra, Zuse developed his own binary system. He accomplished this while he tinkered in his parents' living room on a general-purpose calculating machine based on some of

Charles Babbage's principles. Instead of perforated cards, however, Zuse used strips of 35-millimeter photographic film that had been punched with encoded instructions.

During the 1930s researchers on both sides of the Atlantic Ocean intensified their efforts to improve calculating machines. Initially they were driven by a desire to help engineers, scientists, mathematicians, and others whose work required long, repetitive computations. All too soon, however, these humanistic concerns faded as computer researchers were diverted into making machines for war.

The Impact of World War II

With the outbreak of the Second World War in 1939, automatic computational devices that could be used for military purposes were in big demand in many warring nations. German engineers, for example, used Zuse's ideas to solve aircraft- and missile-design problems. They also utilized the ideas to build radio-controlled aircraft used in combat near the end of the war.

Computer research was also underway in Great Britain, the wartime ally of the United States. Having obtained a replica of the secret German code-sending machine called ENIGMA, British officials set up a specially trained group of scientists and mathematicians in Buckinghamshire, England, to counter the Germans. Their secret mission was to create a massive, electronic, code-breaking computer system called Colossus, which functioned, in part, on the computational ideas conceived by British mathematician Alan Turing. Upon Colossus's completion in 1943, this massive, special-purpose electronic computer decoded almost all secret German radio transmissions made during the war, which helped the Allied nations defeat Germany.

Similar work on computers was underway in the United States. By this time, the United States was deeply involved in the war. Its military forces had a great need for accurate mathematical tables that helped operators of big guns calculate a target's velocity, windspeed, air density, and other factors. Because American armed forces battled their enemies on a variety of geographical areas, they needed a steady supply of up-to-date calculations that reflected the ever-changing conditions of the terrains of war. Their need, however, far exceeded the military's capacity to supply the calculations. Without this crucial data, American gunners were unable to fire many of their large guns during battle.

The military turned to university researchers for help. In 1943, Harvard mathematician Howard Aiken, working with IBM engineers, finished production of the Automatic Sequence Control Calculator, a fifty-one-foot-long, eight-foot-high creation made of glass and stainless steel. The U.S. Navy used this first-ever large-scale automatic digital computer to improve the accuracy of its big guns on moving targets. Each day, the 750,000-part, 35-ton computer, which Aiken nicknamed "Mark One," produced calculations that formerly took mathematicians six months to complete.

The army also sought assistance, but from the University of Pennsylvania. The school had a differential analyzer, like the one at MIT. In addition, it had a group of capable mathematicians who performed many difficult calculations by hand. But when the university effort to provide calculations proved to be slow, army officials sent twenty-nine-year-old Lieutenant Herman Goldstine, a former math professor, to the university to expedite the project. Goldstine soon discovered, however, there was little he could do: The Differential analyzer often broke down and the overworked mathematicians were already working as hard as they could.

A graduate student told Goldstine about the work of John Mauchly, a young engineer on campus. Two years earlier, Mauchly had approached the university's Moore School of Engineering to fund a project that he and his friend J. Presper Eckert had developed: a fully electronic calculating machine with no working parts. Mauchly explained that the machine would be "the electrical analogue of the mechanical adding, multiplying and dividing machines which are now manufactured for ordinary arithmetic purposes."[7] At the time, however, the university's deans had been unimpressed and refused to approve the project. "None of us had much confidence in Mauchly at that time,"[8] recalled a research director at the university.

Howard Aiken and his computer. Completed in 1943, the "Mark One" performed calculations for the U.S. Navy during World War II.

Goldstine, however, *was* impressed with Mauchly after talking with him and convinced that an electronic computer would be fast and accurate enough to produce the mathematical data the army so desperately needed. Next, the army lieutenant persuaded a skeptical panel of military experts to fund the building of ENIAC (Electronic Numerical Integrator and Computer). As the project commenced, the participants experienced a great urgency to succeed. Goldstine later recalled, "We were young and deeply involved. We felt like the whole war depended on us. There was a real sense we were doing something very extraordinary."[9]

Though the war ended before the computer was completed, the project continued. Finally in 1946 it was ready for a trial run. On Valentine's Day, a crowd of two hundred military and government officials, researchers, and journalists gathered to watch. ENIAC's first task was to multiply 97,367 by 5,000. To the astonishment of everyone, the computer produced the answer in a flash. Then just as quickly it squared 13,975.

Next, ENIAC's creators gave it a problem for which the machine was specifically designed: tracking an artillery shell's path of flight. "It [the shell] took 30 seconds to reach its target and the ENIAC computed that tra-

Technicians work on ENIAC, the electronic computer built for the U.S. Army in 1946. ENIAC weighed thirty tons and was nearly the size of a small house.

ENIAC's Amazing Debut

In his book, ENIAC: The Triumphs and Tragedies of the World's First Computer, *author Scott McCartney provides this vivid summary of ENIAC's computing powers.*

What the army got was a thirty-ton monster that filled 18,000 square feet—the size of a three-bedroom apartment in some cities. It had forty different units, including its twenty accumulators, arranged in the shape of a U, sixteen on each side, and eight in the middle, all connected by a ganglion of heavy black cable as thick as fire hose. It was 1,000 times faster than any numerical calculator, 500 times faster than any existing computing machine. It could perform 5,000 additions cycles a second and do the work of 50,000 people working by hand. In thirty seconds, ENIAC could calculate a single trajectory, something that would take twenty hours with a desk calculator or fifteen minutes on the Differential Analyzer. (Today, a supercomputer can perform the same work in three microseconds.)

jectory in about 25 seconds," recalled Arthur Banks, who operated the computer that day. "That was the first time a complex problem had been solved faster than it [the real event] actually took."[10]

Weighing thirty tons and equipped with thirty thousand vacuum tubes, ENIAC was almost the size of a small house. It had required two hundred thousand man hours to construct and cost $486,804. Though the military no longer needed the huge computer to carry out its original purpose, the U.S. government still had a large, powerful machine that was hundreds of times faster than any other calculating device. It could, for example, carry out about five thousand additions and three hundred multiplications per second. Because of ENIAC's amazing computing power, the government assigned it a new task: calculating for the testing of atomic bombs.

Despite its astounding calculating ability, however, ENIAC had its drawbacks. First, it consumed vast amounts of electricity. Electric bills ran as high as $650 an hour, even when the computer was not operating, because electricity was needed to heat up the vacuum tube filaments and keep cooling fans running. Second, ENIAC's vacuum tubes were unreliable. Third, the computer also had to be reprogrammed after each major task, something that often took hours to do.

Nonetheless, ENIAC worked. Considered the world's first digital computer, it represented a stunning development. As Scott McCartney explains, "ENIAC had intelligence. It had the ability to react to data; it was programmable. And for the first time ever, intelligence was all-electronic. Electricity could be used to 'think.'"[11]

FIRST GENERATION COMPUTERS

During the next five years, other large-scale electronic computers appeared in the United States and England. Most of the new machines were faster than ENIAC. They were also more complex and capable of executing many tasks simultaneously. Their memory capacities were improved, too. Thanks to the work of Hungarian-American mathematician John von Neuman, new American-made computers had stored-program capacity. This meant that both the instructions to make a computer work and the data to be processed could be stored in the computer's memory.

Almost all advancements in computer technology during this period were intended to aid military and government projects. But by 1951 Mauchly and Eckert had produced the Universal Automatic Computer (UNIVAC 1), the first commercial computer aimed at the business market. Within six years, forty-five more UNIVAC were built. UNIVAC marked the beginning of what computer engineers later called first generation computers. Other companies with their own computers soon entered this growing market. Among them were IBM, RCA, Sperry Rand, Burroughs, Control Data Corporation, Philco, Honeywell, and

UNIVAC, the first computer intended for business use instead of military or government purposes.

General Electric. All of these companies' machines could computate, read, and write data simultaneously and faster than any other machines in history.

Though vacuum tube-based technology was far superior to any known mechanical calculating system, it had serious limitations. Vacuum tubes were bulky. They burned out too often, broke easily, and generated great amounts of heat. Because of these problems, engineers searched for something better. What they came up with ushered in the era of modern computers.

2 The Rapid Rise of Modern Computing Power

In 1958 researchers at Bell Laboratories invented a replacement for the vacuum tube: the transistor, a tiny electronic marvel that served as a switch for electric currents and paved the way for personal computers.

This new device offered many advantages over the vacuum tube. About 1/200 the size of its predecessor, and made of a solid substance, the transistor generated less heat and was cheaper to produce. It was also more reliable, rugged, and energy efficient.

Early transistors enabled engineers to produce second generation computers that ran faster than ever and had powerful memories stored on magnetic tapes or disks. Some could, for example, multiply two ten-digit numbers in 1/100,000 of a second.

But the impact of transistors was soon overshadowed by a newer and even more powerful technology that developed during the late 1960s and early 1970s. By then computer engineers had learned how to miniaturize electronic components small enough so that hundreds of them fit on a single, tiny silicon chip. Instead of being wired together as earlier circuits using vacuum tubes were, the new circuits—which included tiny transistors and other components such as diodes and resistors—were etched into a single substance, or solid state. These integrated circuits made possible the next generation of computers that surpassed their forerunners.

THE RISE OF INTEGRATED CIRCUITS

By now, a new breed of computer, the minicomputer, had arrived—a product of the ongoing effort to miniaturize computer components. Cheaper and smaller than the large mainframe computers, the minis were also more accessible. But they were still too big. Some were big enough to fill a large bedroom closet. In 1965, Digital Equipment Corporation's PDP-8 minicomputer stood six feet tall and weighed 250 pounds. It also sold for $20,000, a price that was too costly for most individuals. So, most computer users in research labs or business offices had to wait their turn to use a shared computer. Many had to rent computer time. Recalls Microsoft cofounder Bill Gates, "When I was in high school, it cost about $40 an hour to access a time-shared computer using Teletype—for that $40 an hour you got a slice of the computer's precious attention."[12]

Prices did not stay high for very long, however. Within a few years, engineers created yet another generation of computers. Each of these was smaller, cheaper, yet

Microchips, first developed in the late 1960s, consisted of hundreds of miniature electronic components etched into small silicon chips.

thousands of times more powerful than ENIAC, or a score of other earlier generation mainframe computers put together. Known as personal computers (PCs), these amazing machines thrust the Computer Revolution into high gear.

THE ARRIVAL OF THE PC

Today PCs are common pieces of equipment in homes and workplaces in hundreds of countries. Demand for these machines is so great that the personal computer industry is now the third-largest industry in the world. The story of how a machine leapt

from being a top secret military project to a household appliance has no parallel in history. "It happened by accident, because a bunch of disenfranchised nerds [computer zealots] wanted to impress their friends,"[13] suggests Robert Cringely, a chronicler of the computer revolution.

However, what gave these "nerds" the tool they needed to launch the next big phase in the computer revolution was the ever-shrinking computer chip—the microchip. The technology behind the microchip took a huge leap forward in 1971 when Ted Hoff of the Intel Corporation designed a microchip called the 4004. Hailed as the world's first microprocessor, Hoff's creation contained 2,250 individual components that made up the entire central processing unit, or brain, of a computer. All these parts were concentrated onto a single silicon wafer about the size of a human fingernail.

One year later, Intel produced a new microchip, the 8008, which contained 4,500 components. This improved sliver of silicon greatly increased computing speed. Previously, the 4004 chip was able to add two 4-bit numbers in 11 millionths of a second. However, the 8008 could calculate the sum of two 8-bit numbers in 2.5 millionths of a second. (A bit is a binary digit indicated by a 1 or a 0, signifying the presence or absence of an electrical charge. Various combinations of bits represent different numbers.) Continued miniaturization of computer chips hastened the computer revolution over the next few years. Smaller components reduced the size of computers and brought down manufacturing costs, making computers less expensive than ever.

Until the early 1970s computers were not yet commercial products available to the general public. This changed when the January 1975 cover story of *Popular Electronics* magazine announced the arrival of the world's first personal computer. Called the Altair 8800, it had to be built from a do-it-yourself computer kit manufactured by

POPULAR ELECTRONICS ANNOUNCES THE FUTURE

Appearing in Stan Augarten's Bit by Bit: An Illustrated History of Computers, *is this condensed version of the magazine's editor's column explaining the January 1975 cover story.*

For many years, we've been reading and hearing about how computers will one day be a household item. Therefore, we're especially proud to present in this issue the first commercial type of minicomputer project ever published that's priced within reach of many households—the *Altair 8800*, with an under–$400 complete kit cost, including cabinet.

To give you some insight into our editorial goal for this momentous project, we were determined not to present a digital computer demonstrator with blinking LED's [light-emitting diodes] that would simply be fun to build and watch, but suffer from limited usefulness. . . . What we wanted for our readers was a state-of-the-art minicomputer whose capabilities would match those of currently available units at a mere fraction of the cost.

After turning down three computer project proposals that did not meet these requirements, the breakthrough was made possible with the availability of the Intel 8008 . . . the highest-performance, single-chip processor available at this time.

MITS, a calculator company in Albuquerque, New Mexico. Altair's founders hoped to make an affordable computer, though nobody in the company was sure if anybody wanted to buy one.

The Altair housed the Intel 8008 microprocessor, a product Intel never intended to be built into a small retail computer. Nonetheless, when the Altair went on sale in kit form for as little as $397, orders poured in. MITS had hoped to sell eight hundred units in the first year of production, but "a month after it was introduced, we were getting 250 orders a day,"[14] recalls Ed Roberts, a cofounder of the company.

Most of the buyers were electronics hobbyists who had long wanted their own computers. Few of them, though, had any idea of what to do with their new possessions. After all, the Altair had no monitor, printer, or keyboard. Input of data was done manually by throwing sixteen switches, a cumbersome process. Output was also primitive by modern standards. Solutions to simple math problems, for example, were indicated by a series of glowing light bulbs.

Despite these limitations, many budding computerists realized that the Altair was something special. Among these admirers were Bill Gates, then a nineteen-year-old Harvard student, and his long-time friend, Paul Allen. Though excited about the Altair, the two believed the computer was less than desirable in its present form. As Gates recalls, "Part of the problem was that the Altair 8800 lacked software. It couldn't be programmed, which made it more a novelty than a tool."[15]

The two young men decided to fix the problem themselves and perhaps make some money. Gates recalls, "I wanted to be involved from the beginning. The chance to get in on the first stages of the PC revolution seemed the opportunity of a lifetime, and I seized it."[16] So, in 1977, Gates dropped out of Harvard University and helped Allen write BASIC (Beginner All-Purpose Symbolic Instruction Code) language programs that turned the Altair into a computer that did real work. (Three years later, this partnership evolved into a small, thirty-two-employee company in Bellevue, Washington, that won a contract to produce computer programs for IBM's new PC. The company was called Microsoft and in time it became one of the most profitable companies in history.)

Others took note of Altair's success, and by the end of the 1970s dozens of new companies with names such as Kim Vip, Elf, and Imsai were also manufacturing mail-order computer kits. Says Altair's Ed Roberts, "We created an industry. I think that goes completely unnoticed. . . . Every aspect of the industry . . . software, hardware, applications stuff, dealerships, you name it."[17]

Initially, however, almost everyone who owned an early PC was looking for a way to make it useful. To generate ideas and to socialize with like-minded people, many of the computer owners formed clubs. One club that was destined to become famous was the Homebrew Computer Club, which met in a rented hall at Stanford University in California. Here, computer owners shared computing tips and displayed new computer applications or other homemade electronic devices.

Though members of the Homebrew Computer Club came from all walks of life,

Microsoft's Humble Beginning

In his book The Road Ahead, *entrepreneur and software engineer Bill Gates recalls how he and his friend Paul Allen began a company that later became known as Microsoft.*

In 1975, when Paul and I naively decided to start a company, we were acting like characters in all those Judy Garland and Mickey Rooney movies who crowed, "We'll put on a show in the barn!" There was no time to waste. Our first project was to create BASIC for the little computer [the Altair 8800].

We had to squeeze a lot of capability into the computer's small memory. The typical Altair had about 4,000 characters of memory. Today most personal computers have 4 or 8 million characters of memory. Our task was further complicated because we didn't actually own an Altair, and had never even seen one. That didn't really matter because what we were really interested in was the new Intel 8080 microprocessor chip, and we'd never seen that, either. Undaunted, Paul studied a manual for the chip, then wrote a program that made a big computer at Harvard mimic the little Altair. This was like having a whole orchestra available and using it to play a simple duet, but it worked.

Writing good software requires a lot of concentration, and writing BASIC for the Altair was exhausting. Sometimes I rock back and forth or pace when I'm thinking, because it helps me focus on a single idea and exclude distractions. I did a lot of rocking and pacing in my dorm room the winter of 1975. Paul and I didn't sleep much and lost track of night and day. When I did fall asleep, it was often at my desk or on the floor. Some days I didn't eat or see anyone. But after five weeks, our BASIC was written—and the world's first microcomputer software company was born. In time we named it "Microsoft."

Bill Gates started his microcomputer software company in 1975.

many were entrenched in California's counterculture, which advocated nonconformity, antimaterialism, and alternative lifestyles. One of the counterculture's most cherished values was an emphasis on communal sharing—a practice that took root at club meetings. "Everybody was sharing [their ideas about computers]. Everybody won," [18] says Jim Waren, a former social activist in the 1960s, and founder of the West Coast Computer Faire, once the world's largest computer show.

Attending these meetings were two recent graduates of a local high school— Steve Wozniak and Steve Jobs, the future founders of Apple Corporation. They too were affected by the radical, creative climate of the day. Recalls Jobs: "The spark of that was that there was something beyond . . . what you see every day. . . . It's the same thing that causes people to want to be poets instead of bankers. . . . And I think that same spirit can be put into products." [19]

The first electronic device Wozniak and Jobs built together, however, was not inspired by poetic sensibility, but prankishness. They called it a blue box and its main purpose was to allow its users to cheat telephone companies by using special dial tones to make long distance telephone calls for free.

Even though the blue box was meant to defraud, it worked. And this fact gave Jobs and Wozniak the confidence to build something more legitimate and useful. "What we learned," says Jobs, "was that we could build something ourselves that could control billions of dollars worth of infrastructure in the world. . . . That was an incredible lesson. I don't think there would ever have been an Apple Computer had there not been blue boxing." [20]

THE CREATION OF APPLE COMPUTERS

In 1976 the two young men launched their next project—a personal computer, designed by Wozniak, called Apple I. This time Jobs and Wozniak intended to make money off their work. But the PC failed to attract many hobbyists when it went on sale. This did not discourage the two friends, however, because by now they sensed that an even bigger computer market was developing across the nation. Jobs remembers thinking that for every hobbyist willing to put a computer kit together, "there were a thousand people who couldn't do that . . . but wanted to mess around with programming." [21]

Apple Corporation president John Scully (center) with company founders Steve Jobs (left) and Steve Wozniak (right) in 1984.

With this view in mind, Jobs and Wozniak built a new kind computer for the general consumer market. Called the Apple II, it was the first-ever completely assembled PC, complete with color graphics. When the Apple II made its debut in 1977, it became an instant hit. Thousands of orders poured into the company, and by 1980 the Apple Corporation employed several thousand workers to keep up with the growing demand.

As Apple computers received rave reviews across the country, other companies entered the growing retail market with their own PCs. One of the most successful was Commodore, begun by Jack Tramiel, a survivor of a Nazi concentration camp who immigrated to the United States. Tandy Radio Shack, a Texas-based chain of stores, sold Commadore's PCs alongside its other specialty electronic products.

Despite this burst of competition, Apple controlled more than 50 percent of the market, and by 1980 it remained the clear industry leader. The company's sudden success, and the PC industry it had helped to spawn, was stunning. Five years previously almost no one had a personal computer; now a $1 billion PC industry existed. Industry analysts confidently predicted that with increasing numbers of people wanting the new devices, PC sales could only soar.

A COMPUTER GIANT ENTERS THE PC MARKET

The sudden popularity of the PC did not go unnoticed by another computer manufacturer—a well-known corporate giant that

Within a few years of its introduction in 1981, the IBM PC dominated the market.

previously had paid little attention to the idea of building computers for home use. But in 1981, IBM shook up the PC world by announcing its own line of personal computers. Because the company was late in entering the competition, it had to build its PC quickly. Company officials decided the best way to do this was to adopt a new market strategy.

With its other large-scale computer products, IBM had used its own unique, or proprietary, system that no other company could copy without permission. Because IBM dominated so much of the market for mainframe and minicomputers, the company's customers had almost no choice other than IBM from which to buy computers, software, replacement parts, and service.

But to successfully market its PC, IBM chose a different path. Its engineers put together a computer with parts that were already widely available on the open market. For example, it used a 16-bit microchip from Intel and an operating system designed by

Microsoft. Explains Bill Gates, "IBM elected to build its PC mainly from off-the-shelf components available to anyone. This made a platform that was fundamentally open, which made it easy to copy." [22]

IBM's decision to use this open architecture allowed other manufacturers to build clones—computers that closely resembled IBMs. Instead of hurting IBM's sales, however, these clones actually benefitted IBM in the long run, because they helped establish the IBM format as the industry standard for the personal computer.

The wisdom of IBM's decision became apparent when powerful rivals such as Xerox, Texas Instruments, Hewlett Packard, and DEC followed IBM into the retail computer market. Each of these companies sold its own version of a PC that operated on a unique operating system. This meant, for example, that software designed for the Xerox family of computers did not run on IBM's or any other manufacturers' machines.

Meanwhile, IBM owners could buy software and replacement parts from numerous sources that also supplied owners of IBM clones. This universality of service and parts gave IBM a competitive edge over Apple and others. By the mid-1980s, most computer companies whose PCs did not operate on the IBM platform had disappeared from the market. The only remaining significant alternative to the IBM system was the Apple II PC.

FIGHTING FOR DOMINANCE

Competition between Apple and IBM intensified during the next few years and helped to bring many new computer products to market. In 1984, Apple introduced a very new type of computer—the Macintosh, or Mac. This newcomer made use of a new technology pioneered by researchers at the Xerox Corporation. Called Graphical User Interface, or GUI, this software gave users a new way to send commands to a PC, rather than typing them on a keyboard. Instead, computerists could now activate various computer programs using a handheld device called a mouse to click on colorful icons that appeared on the monitor screen.

In 1985, IBM responded by marketing new computers that used Microsoft's new GUI Windows operating system. Now IBM users could also use a mouse to click on icons. They could also run several programs simultaneously.

During the next few years, other computer products appeared. Among them were portable laptop PCs with lightweight batteries and liquid crystal display monitors. Computers that could operate as facsimile, or fax, machines also hit the market. And so did scanners—devices that optically read printed material and converted it into stored data into computers.

By the early 1990s a standard for home computing equipment had emerged. It consisted of a central processing unit, a monitor, audio speakers, a keyboard, a mouse, and a printer. Most systems also came equipped with a modem—a device that allowed computers to send and receive data from other computers connected by telephone lines.

PC systems were powerful, easy to use, and affordable—most costing $1500 or less.

STEVE JOBS LUCKS OUT

In PC World, *writer Harry McCracken tells how Apple Corporation's Steven Jobs came across the idea of GUI while visiting a Xerox lab and changed the course of personal computing.*

Some folks say Steve Jobs pulled the heist of the century when he struck a deal with Xerox in 1979. The firm could invest $1 million in Apple if Jobs could visit its Palo Alto Research Center. Xerox said yes, and a Pandora's box swung open.

At PARC, Jobs spied the Alto, an experimental PC with a Graphical User Interface. Within minutes, it's been reported, Jobs realized that in the future, all computers would use a GUI.

According to conventional wisdom, Apple then cloned the Alto with its Macintosh—before Microsoft, in turn, mimicked the Mac with Windows. But Apple's work on the Mac had already begun when Jobs toured Xerox. And Jef Raskin, an Apple employee, had been exploring graphical interfaces as early as 1967. "The only thing [Apple] took," says historian Owen W. Linzmayer, "was inspiration." Indeed, the company was solely responsible for many elements of the modern GUI, including the clipboard, trash can, and drag-and-drop file management—making the visit to PARC seem like something less than grand larceny.

Apple founder Steve Jobs instantly recognized the potential of Graphical User Interface (GUI).

Store shelves brimmed with scores of useful software packages. All of this was good news to the public that continued to embrace PCs with zeal. Personal computers, it seemed, could be used at home and work for any number of purposes. Year after year, growing numbers of people from many walks of life purchased PCs and used them

in ways the pioneers of the computer revolution had never dreamed possible.

PCs BECOME UNIVERSAL

By the early 1990s, PCs were found almost everywhere in the industrialized world. They appeared in homes, offices, factories, schools, churches, farms, department stores, police precincts, courthouses, airports, and many other places.

Word processing became one of the most common uses for the PC. No longer were journalists, secretaries, advertisers, and correspondents dependent on typewriters, carbon paper, and correction fluid. Now their PCs allowed them to compose letters and manuscripts on a computer screen and print out hard copies. PCs also provided speedy help with office chores such as billing, accounting, pricing, inventory making, record keeping, and business planning.

Millions of PC owners also used their new machines for entertainment purposes. By far the most popular application was computer games. Adventure, action, and fantasy entertainments, along with games of skill, luck, and trivia, enthralled millions.

School systems across the United States and elsewhere caught the PC fever. Convinced that students needed computer skills to survive in the ever-changing workplace, schools from kindergarten to the university level added computer literacy courses to their curricula. School officials also encouraged the use of special educational software

Office workers were much aided by the advent of word processing. PCs also revolutionized other tasks such as accounting and record keeping.

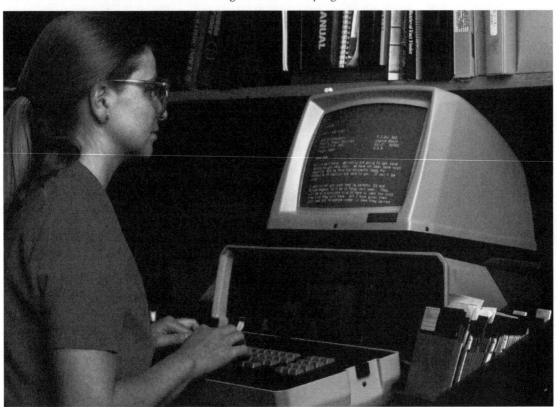

programs, designed to help students master basic skills in math and reading.

PCs also boosted creative talents. Using special software, many composers learned to compose music upon electronic keyboards as the correct notations appeared on the monitor. To change musical keys, add special effects, or blend parts of other songs into the composition required only a few mouse clicks. Choreographers of big productions also discovered that PCs could help them create and display routines of hundreds of onstage dancers. Graphic artists made PCs part of their kit of tools, too. Animation, product design, advertising layouts, and other artistic tasks were all made easier with computers.

In recent years, movie makers have entertained millions of viewers around the world with breathtakingly realistic computer-generated images of dinosaurs, mammoths, and creatures never before imagined. PC software also allowed studio artists to morph real-life objects into computer enhanced images. This technique, plus other special effects made possible by PCs, have enabled film makers to create these startlingly realistic illusions.

SUPER COMPUTERS

As PCs grew in popularity, demand remained steady for an older member of the computer family: the supercomputer. Used mainly for scientific and military purposes, the supercomputer had also become a fast and powerful machine that revolutionized scientific experimentation in physics and in other scientific fields.

Though many people contributed to the development of this large-scale, hyper-fast machine, one man stands out: Seymor Cray. Obsessed with a lifelong desire to make computers faster and faster, Cray, along with business partner William Norris, founded the Control Data Company (CDC) in 1957. Because other computer manufacturers dominated the business market at the time, Cray and Norris instead focused on building big and very fast computers needed to crunch large numbers quickly in scientific laboratories. One of CDC's first creations was the 1604, a computer that used transistors instead of vacuum tubes. By 1964, Cray's new creation, the CDC 6600, became the world's fastest computer. Its speed, measured at 3 million floating-point operations per second (FLOPS), inspired admirers to christen it a "supercomputer." For a while, CDC pushed aside IBM and became the industry leader in manufacturing supercomputers.

After an argument with Norris, however, Cray left CDC in 1972 to start Cray Research, another company that built even faster supercomputers. Others soon joined the field, including W. Daniel Hillis, a graduate student at MIT who pioneered a new way of supercomputing. His idea was to network several smaller microprocessors—rather than use one central processor—to achieve supercomputing speeds comparable to that of Cray's computers. In 1983, Hillis helped to set up the Thinking Machines Corporation, which built and marketed multiprocessor supercomputers.

Supercomputers have been used primarily for military purposes. They were put to work, for example, in 1996, when the

United States signed the Comprehensive Test Ban Treaty, which put restrictions on the testing of nuclear weapons. Instead of detonating real bombs, the U.S. Department of Energy turned to supercomputers to simulate the testing of nuclear weapons. To accomplish this, a supercomputer had to be able to perform 100 trillion FLOPS.

By this time, supercomputers were also being used in other fields such as the petroleum, aerospace, and automotive industries. Supercomputers helped meteorologists predict the weather. Questions in physics concerning subatomic particles and the creation of the universe were also being addressed by supercomputers by the late 1990s.

Meanwhile, PCs continued to become more efficient and powerful, and increasingly proved themselves capable of handling many tasks that once were performed by supercomputers alone. What made this trend possible was the constant improvement in chip technology. By the turn of the twenty-first century, microchips—the computer brains—had become as ubiquitous as personal computers.

THE EVER-PRESENT COMPUTER CHIP

Because they are cheap and powerful, microprocessors are now standard parts in automobiles, surgical and diagnostic equipment, televisions, fax machines, printers, elevators, cash machines, video cameras, digital telephones, children's toys, home entertainment systems, and even some toasters and refrigerators. Microchips also lie at the heart of the most sophisticated aircraft, missiles, bombs,

and detection systems. Even inexpensive drug store Christmas cards may now come imbedded with a tiny chip that plays carols when the cards are opened. In 1982 people around the world were astonished when American physician Robert Jarvik successfully installed an artificial heart controlled by a microprocessor into the chest of Dr. Barney Clark, allowing the patient to live for 112 days.

Tiny computer chips also make possible a new phenomenon: telepresence. Robotized mechanisms loaded with microprocessors are capable of receiving radio signals from remote areas and carrying out various tasks, whether the machines are in a dangerous mine, on an ocean floor, or on the surface of Mars.

Experiments with telemedicine were achieved in recent years when physicians began exploring the use of computers and advanced communications technologies to interview and examine patients located thousands of miles away. Some physicians even imagine a future when they will be able to perform surgery from a distance, using television and surgical equipment embedded with microchips.

As technology for telepresence devices unfolded, many builders began using microchips in new construction projects to produce an array of so-called "smart buildings," ranging from corporate offices to new homes. These structures are designed to detect input from humans and act upon it. Embedded chips in walls, for instance, enable thermostats to sense the room for human body heat and adjust the room temperature and electric lighting accordingly.

Mars rovers are equipped with microprocessors to receive and execute commands sent via radio signal by scientists on Earth.

As microchip technology advances, many computer experts expect to see chips imbedded not only in appliances and mechanisms, but also in everyday items such as personal clothing to provide constant data to computers anywhere about an individual's whereabouts, activities, and personal needs during the day. What will make it possible for computers to receive such input is an immense communications system, already in existence, that is unlike any other in history. It is called the Internet.

3 The Third Wave: Linking the Computers of the World

The Internet is a vast worldwide communications system consisting of telephone lines and radio networks linking hundreds of millions of computers around the globe. Unlike all previous communication media, it allows its users to communicate by text, video, voice, and code. Vast amounts of information can be accessed from Internet sites created by museums, businesses, research labs, universities, associations, governments, political groups, and millions of individuals worldwide. In addition, this information can be stored, reorganized, and sent to others around the world.

Like the modern computer, the Internet has no single inventor or creator. Instead, it is the product of the inspired work of hundreds of men and women. And like the modern computer, it, too, was a byproduct of military research.

THE EARLY DAYS

When World War II ended in 1945, the United States faced a new enemy—its former ally, the Soviet Union. Opposing ideologies and mutual suspicion fueled an arms race between the nations that lasted decades. American fears intensified when in 1956 the Soviets successfully launched the world's first artificial satellite into orbit around the earth. Many Americans worried that the Soviet's superior space technology could also be used to make better weapons and endanger the United States and its allies.

In response, the U.S. Department of Defense's Advanced Research Projects Agency (ARPA) funded several research programs at major universities, government labs, and defense contractors aimed at improving the nation's weapons and radar systems. ARPA officials soon realized, however, that their computers were inadequate for their ever-increasing workloads. So, they funded a $1 million experimental computer network called ARPAnet that used telephone lines to link university and research sites around the country. Once ARPAnet was up and running, researchers and scientists hoped to share data and perform high-level computing tasks on remote supercomputers.

The technology behind ARPAnet was partly based on a concept advanced in 1960 by Paul Baran, a researcher for the Rand Corporation, a nonprofit military think tank in California. Though Baran's idea was never put into use as he intended, it would later contribute to the ideas that created the Internet.

At the time, officials within the U.S. military establishment worried that the nation was incapable of protecting its government and keeping military communication lines open during a nuclear attack. Baran proposed a solution based on two key ideas. First, he suggested doing away with the current military communication system, which consisted of a few large centers that served as hubs, and several smaller ones scattered around the country. Baran pointed out that the entire system would stop working if any one of the hubs was destroyed in an attack. Instead, he advanced the idea of a new communication system made up of many small sites, or nodes. Instead of hubs, all nodes had equal importance. This meant each site had the capability to originate, receive, and pass along all communication signals to all other nodes. In theory, they resembled points on a net: If any site was destroyed in a nuclear attack, all other undamaged nodes could keep communication lines open.

This led to Baran's second idea of how communications signals were sent. He believed the military should not transmit complete signals from one site to the next. Instead, computers should break up the messages into small portions of data. Next, copies of these chunks of information would be sent to all the other nodes, each taking a different route. In this way, if one site was damaged by an enemy attack, parts of the disassembled message were still intact somewhere. Once all these chopped-up portions arrived at their final destination, computers would reassemble them into the original message.

As intriguing as Baran's ideas were, however, they failed to generate interest among the military establishment and were never used to build a new military communication system. Discouraged, Baran gave up on his ideas in 1965 and went to work on other assignments. About this same time, however, English physicist Donald Davies, working independently, also came up with the concept of breaking up computer messages. He called the idea packet switching—a name that stuck.

Several years later, ARPAnet officials thought packet switching ideas were ideal for improving their computer-sharing network. Among other things, Baran's concept allowed computers linked to other computers to use telephone lines more efficiently. Instead of transmitting a steady stream of

The Soviet Union's 1957 launch of Sputnik I *(pictured) prompted the United States to upgrade its defense systems.*

data, computers send out bursts of electronic information with wasteful microsecond pauses in between. Packet switching, however, offered a way to send data from other computers during these pauses. This efficient use of time allowed several computers to share the same telephone line almost simultaneously.

ARPANET TESTS PACKET SWITCHING

By 1969, ARPAnet's engineers had built a packet switching communication system and were ready to test it. They chose four sites for a trial run: the University of California campuses at Los Angeles (UCLA) and Santa Barbara (UCSB), Stanford Research Institute (SRI), and the University of Utah. All four campuses were connected with a network of transmission lines and computers assembled by Bolt, Beranke and Newman (BBN), a Cambridge, Massachusetts, firm.

The system proved successful when the sites at UCLA and SRI swapped data. A month later all four university sites were communicating with each other. By 1971, ARPAnet had fifteen nodes; a year later thirty-seven were connected. The foundation for what would one day be called the Internet had been laid.

GOING PERSONAL

Because the U.S. government had established ARPAnet to carry out serious scientific and military-related research work, network officials restricted how the system could be used. This meant ARPAnet users were under instructions to use the network only to share scientific information with other researchers, or to carry out computations on remote computers. They could not use the network for personal reasons, such as sending private messages to one another. Although security reasons played a big role in this decision, some supervisors also feared that sending private electronic mail, or e-mail, could violate U.S. postal regulations. "You'll be in jail in no time,"[23] Paul Baran warned his fellow workers.

All too soon ARPAnet administrators realized their policy was hard to enforce. Numerous authorized users—many of them university graduate students—ignored the restrictions and used the network to send one another personal correspondence, gossip, and trivia about a wide range of nonmilitary matters. "People to people communications ... [not] machine to machine or human to machine,"[24] excited people the most, says Len Kleinrock, a UCLA engineer involved in ARPAnet.

When other university graduate students heard about ARPAnet, they decided to build a computer network for themselves. In 1979 three graduate students at the University of North Carolina and Duke University set up a network they called USEnet. At first, students primarily used the new system for research purposes. Soon, however, personal e-mail flowed back and forth between the two campuses. Several USEnet users also formed on-line discussion groups, or newsgroups, and exchanged electronic messages that expressed commentary on a wide range of topics.

More networks soon appeared. The City University of New York along with Yale University in New Haven, Connecticut, for

Len Kleinrock, of the University of California at Los Angeles, was one of the engineers who worked on ARPAnet, the forerunner of the Internet.

instance, created the "Because It's There" network (BITnet). The main purpose of this network was to provide on-line access to other universities not involved in military research. Meanwhile, several other universities, along with the Rand Corporation and BBN, formed the Science Network (CSNET). Xerox's Palo Alto Research Center (PARC) was also connected.

In 1986, The Cleveland Free Net was up and running and available to the public at no charge. Similar "freenets" appeared elsewhere nationwide. During this time, USEnet kept expanding. By then the network had linked its users with faraway sites in Europe and Australia.

LETTING COMPUTERS TALK TO EACH OTHER

Although many of these far-flung computer networks used different designs and specifications, users could still communicate with one another because their computers used a software called TCP/IP. The need for such a program had first become apparent during ARPAnet's debut in 1969. Computers at the four university test sites could communicate because their clock speeds, packet sizes, and other features were all built to the same specifications. Scientists realized, however, that linking other computers built to different specifications would be more difficult.

Vinton Cerf co-developed TCP, protocols that allow computers to share files and communicate with other networks.

In 1973 computer scientist Vinton Cerf and MIT math professor Robert Kahn came up with a solution. It was a set of software properties, or protocols, called TCP (Transmission Control Protocol), which enabled dissimilar types of computers to share computer files. Better yet, these protocols also allowed computer users to communicate with different computer networks anywhere in the world.

Researchers tested TCP for the first time in July 1977. Using funds provided by the U.S. Department of Defense, researchers attempted to link ARPAnet with two new communication networks. One was Hawaii-based ALOHAnet, a network that connected computers at different sites by using radio signals that bounced off orbiting satellites. The other was another satellite-based communication system—SATnet, which linked computers in Europe and North America.

The trial message began its ninety-four thousand-mile journey as a radio signal sent from a computer in a van traveling on a highway near San Francisco. Almost instantly the message arrived at a site in Massachusetts, where it was beamed via satellite to Norway. The message next traveled to University College in London. From there it was beamed back by satellite to ARPAnet and followed a ground line to a site at the University of Southern California.

Considered by many to be the birth of the Internet, this successful experiment was only the beginning. Much more work remained to be done before a worldwide computer network could operate efficiently. The next big breakthrough came a year later when engineers at the Xerox Corporation enhanced the TCP software by adding another program called Internet Protocol (IP) that allowed the routing of individual messages. Together

TCP/IP provided the software that makes the modern Internet possible.

A NEW NETWORK EVOLVES

As the number of networks and links proliferated, ARPAnet diminished in importance. In 1983 it split into two separate networks. The federal government designated one of them as MILnet, and set it aside solely for military purposes. The second network linked to other networks, including USEnet and NSFnet, which was created by the National Science Foundation. This amalgam of networks eventually became known as the Internet.

Soon, other government agencies, along with many groups in the general public, obtained access to TCP/IP software, making it possible for more and more existing networks to link together. Organizations such as the National Aeronautics and Space Administration (NASA), the National Institutes of Health (NIH), and various corporations, each with its own powerful computers, formed their own networks and wired them to the Internet. By the start of 1989 more than eighty thousand host computers had connected to the growing network.

In that same year, U.S. government engineers took what was left of ARPAnet off-line forever, an act that symbolized the growing importance of the Internet. Though few paid attention to the demise of a network that launched a communication revolution, Vinton Cerf paid his respects by writing a requiem: "Now pause with me a moment, shed some/tears./ For auld lang syne, for love, for years and years/of faithful service,

duty done, I weep./ Lay down thy packet, now, O friend, and sleep."[25]

In 1991, the fledgling Internet received a big boost when the U.S. Congress approved the National Research and Education Network (NREN), a $2 billion project aimed at upgrading the Internet over the next five years.

THE WEB

As these developments unfolded in the United States, another project neared completion in Europe that would soon make the Internet accessible to the world. Earlier in 1989, Tim Berners-Lee, a British computer programmer at the European Laboratory for Particle Physics, reached a decision that changed the course of history. Like many others in his field, Berners-Lee was frustrated that he and his colleagues around the world who did research for CERN (the Geneva, Switzerland-based European center for Nuclear Research), used incompatible computers that made sharing data with each other nearly impossible.

Berners-Lee tackled the problem by creating special software that linked the software and hardware of CERN's worldwide community of computers. He called his operating system the World Wide Web (WWW), or simply the Web. He chose this name because he hoped his creation would one day link the computers of the world.

The design of the Web consisted of three separate software programs. The first is known today as Universal Resource Locators (URLs); its main function is to help computer messages find their destination.

Dreaming of the Web

In his book, Weaving the Web, *Tim Berners-Lee, explains his ultimate dream for the Internet.*

Tim Berners-Lee, inventor of the World Wide Web.

When I first began tinkering with a software program that eventually gave rise to the idea of the World Wide Web, I named it Enquire, short for *Enquire Within upon Everything,* a musty old book of Victorian advice I noticed as a child in my parents' house outside London. With its title suggestive of magic, the book served as a portal to a world of information, everything from how to remove clothing stains to tips on investing money. Not a perfect analogy for the Web, but a primitive starting point.

What that first bit of Enquire code led me to was something much larger, a vision encompassing the decentralized, organic growth of ideas, technology, and society. The vision I have for the Web is about anything being potentially connected with anything. It is a vision that provides us with new freedom, and allows us to grow faster than we ever could when we were fettered by the hierarchical classification systems into which we bound ourselves. It leaves the entirety of our previous ways of working as just one tool among many. And it brings the workings of society closer to the workings of our mind.

The second is HTTP or Hypertext Transfer Protocol—a program that instructs computers how to display a certain page of text and how to link pages of various sites to exchange text, audio, video, and other data. With this powerful software almost any information that is changed to digital form can be transmitted over cables or radio waves to destinations almost anywhere in the world. The third program is based on Hypertext Markup Language (HTML), a language that is particularly good at displaying documents and making hyperlinks—connections within an electronic document to another document located elsewhere on-line.

Initially, only CERN researchers had access to the software. Then in 1991 the research institute made it available to the world for free. The software package also included another program Berners-Lee designed. It was a GUI-based browser that allows users to click on icons to search for specific documents on the Internet.

Berners-Lee worried that his idea of linking the computers of the world with software might not prevail. "At any point, we were waiting for something to happen—a competing commercial product to knock it out of existence or a competing Internet service to knock it out of existence,"[26] he recalls.

Instead, the World Wide Web grew in popularity around the globe. As it did, entrepreneurs flooded Berners-Lee with various business proposals to exploit the Internet for profit. He rejected them all. Instead, he favored making the software widely available, so that no one corporation or group could dominate the Internet. Something more than money appealed to him. He recalls, "The fact that the World Wide Web did work—I find it not just exciting for itself, but exciting for the whole idea that you can have an idea . . . and it can happen. It means that dreamers all over the world should take heart and not stop."[27]

In this spirit, Berners-Lee also encouraged software programmers everywhere to come up with their own browsers that could improve on his software. Among the first to accept his challenge were two programmers at the University of Illinois National Center for Supercomputing Application, Marc Andreessen and Eric Bina. They led a team that developed software called Mosaic, another point-and-click browser with graphics that made the Internet easier to navigate and paved the way for millions of users to go online.

In those early days, many engineers and researchers shared Berners-Lee's philoso-phy of keeping the Internet free of commercial purpose. Michael Folk, a researcher who worked on the Mosaic project, comments on the spirit of cooperation that existed during the Web's infancy: "What amazed me during the early days was the enormous amount of free energy that went into developing that technology. People from all over the world contributed huge amounts of time and ideas in a surprisingly non-competitive, collaborative way."[28]

Nonetheless, the commercialization of the Internet was on the way. In 1994, Andreessen and Bina joined a new company called Netscape and produced an even better graphical browser called Navigator, which it licensed to industry. Within two years, the

Marc Andreessen introduced the computer world to two browsers: Mosaic and Navigator.

young company was reporting annual revenues of $340 million. The next year revenues hit $500 million.

Such earnings caught the attention of Microsoft, which introduced its own browser, Internet Explorer, in 1995. Unlike Netscape, however, Microsoft offered use of its product for free. This move forced Netscape to do the same. Soon, there was fierce competition between the two companies.

Although both companies were giving away their software, they still made money. Advertising, marketing data, file management, and other specialized Internet services now made up much of the business for Netscape and Microsoft. This business model became a standard for many other new Internet-based companies that soon offered a host of other on-line products. Among the most popular were e-mail programs that enabled computer users to transmit electronic letters worldwide. Various search engines pioneered by startup companies such as Yahoo!, Web Crawler, Lycos, Alta Vista, and Excite, also appeared on the Internet in the mid-1990s and provided millions of computer users with powerful on-line tools.

By this time, the Internet was no longer primarily a medium for researchers and scientists. It was also fast becoming a major medium for business. Although businesses and trade organizations were not allowed on the Internet, many had already formed their own private computer networks and were eager to tie their systems to the Internet. But before this could happen, U.S. law had to be changed. Existing federal regulations forbid using the Internet for anything except official business such as scientific research. This re-

striction vanished in 1992 when U.S. Representative Frederick Boucher, from the ninth district of Virginia, successfully introduced legislation that amended the National Science Foundation Act, and paved the way for opening up the Internet for commercial purposes. By 1994 many new commercial services such as the Internet Shopping Network were on-line. Banks and mail-order companies soon followed. Radio stations began advertising and broadcasting over the new worldwide communication system.

Businesses were not the only big organizations that went on-line. Governments also recognized the potential of the Internet. In 1993 both the White House and the United Nations created websites. Congress set up its own Web pages, too.

Soon, local, regional, and national governments all over the world created websites and posted laws, minutes, legal documents, tax information, and many other kinds of public information. University libraries, public schools, research centers, think tanks, political parties, unions, trade groups, advocacy groups, and almost every interest group imaginable also made their views known to the world on the Internet.

During this time, then U.S. vice president Al Gore publicly championed the Internet in his speeches. Increasingly, he popularized the term "Information Superhighway" to describe the Internet. Some writers say writer Ralph Lee Smith first came up with expression in *The Nation* magazine. Regardless of the source, the metaphor became common in everyday speech, as writers and media commentators discussed exits, on-ramps, and roadkills on the Information Superhighway.

AL GORE CHRISTENS THE INFORMATION HIGHWAY

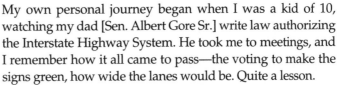

A popular misconception in the United States is that former Vice President Al Gore took credit for "inventing the internet." Gore denies ever having said this, but he does say he popularized the term for the Internet as the "Information Superhighway." During this excerpt from an interview with journalists of Yahoo, Internet Life *Vice President Al Gore relates how he came up with the name.*

My own personal journey began when I was a kid of 10, watching my dad [Sen. Albert Gore Sr.] write law authorizing the Interstate Highway System. He took me to meetings, and I remember how it all came to pass—the voting to make the signs green, how wide the lanes would be. Quite a lesson.

See, I grew up with a dad who was in Congress for 32 years, so I think I developed an overemphasis on the role government played in making things happen. Later, when I got to college, I saw in my studies how technology was often a bigger force for change than any government decisions. That's what I majored in, in college: studying the interaction of technology and democracy. My thesis was about the effect of TV on the constitutional system. And it was during that time that I looked at what was starting to happen with computers.

By the time I got to Congress in '76, I began holding these hearings about the future. What I realized then was that the phenomenon later to be known as Moore's Law [the prediction that transistor capacity would double every eighteen months] was causing a logarithmic increase in processing power, and yet the throughput capacity was hardly changing at all.

For me, that harked back to the lesson I'd learned at the age of 10, when I heard my dad explain how the sudden proliferation of cars after World War II would overwhelm our two-lane superhighway systems. Well, in the mid '70s, I was seeing the same thing begin to happen with information, and so we needed an *information* superhighway. Information was expanding beyond the capacity of our two-lane information road—the twisted copper pair [phone lines]. That's when I started evangelizing about the ideas of an information superhighway. . . . In Japan in the early '90s, they published a book with my face on the cover, a collection of my speeches on this, and they called it *The Information Superhighway.*

Al Gore speaks to elementary school students about the Internet.

Information for All

As the Internet expanded in the mid-1990s, millions of individuals went on-line to explore the vast supply of offerings. Getting connected, however, was not an easy task. Unlike big institutions, most individual PC users lacked the software and hardware resources to make the necessary connections. For help they turned to new companies such as Compuserve, Excite, America On-line, or telephone and cable companies, all of which became known as Internet Service Providers, or ISPs.

Though the Internet was an American creation, it soon became a world phenomenon.

By 1996, 134 countries enjoyed full Internet access, according to the Internet Society. In addition, another 52 nations had limited access, usually in the form of e-mail. Four years later an estimated 100 million users were on-line. Some observers believe that 1 billion people may have Internet access by 2005.

Within a decade the Internet had become a worldwide communication medium that breathed new life into the computer revolution. Access to the Internet combined with an ordinary household PC bestowed upon human beings a level of personal power never before known. What they did with this power forever changed the world, for better and for worse.

4 A Changing Society

The ongoing Computer Revolution has done more than merely equip hundreds of millions of people with a new technology. It also changed the world by affecting the lives of individuals and the larger society in which they lived. Perhaps its greatest impact has been on the distribution of power within society.

For thousands of years, the flow of information in most societies was controlled by small groups of people. Religions, governments, universities, research labs, news organizations, business groups, and corporations have all been guardians of vital information. A half century ago, their control was strengthened by the arrival of large, mainframe computers. During this early phase of the Computer Revolution, in fact, those who had access to these machines had even greater control than their predecessors over the collection, organization, and dissemination of information.

But the rise of PCs in the 1980s and 1990s signalled a change in how information was managed. Personal computers offered computing power that rivaled and even surpassed most large mainframe computers of not too long ago. In addition, the emergence of the Internet, which no government

can yet effectively control, also allowed PC users to tap millions of data banks worldwide. Never before has any other technology bestowed so much personal power upon ordinary human beings as the PC and the Internet have. Ed Roberts, the inventor of the Altair, the world's first PC, explains: "When you talk about power, what you're really saying is 'How many people do you control?' If I were to give you an army of 10,000 people, could you build a pyramid? A computer gives the average person . . . the power to do things in a week that all the mathematicians who ever lived until thirty years ago couldn't do."[29]

The combined impact of the PC and the Internet have had a far-reaching effect on society. Together, they are breaking up, or decentralizing, the concentration of power once held by small numbers of people in almost all the nations of the world. Observes *Newsweek*'s technology writer Steven Levy:

> For many years [large, mainframe] computers were thought to be a centralizing force—those in the upper levels of a hierarchy could access up-to-date files on millions of people and . . . [spy on them]. But since the advent of personal computers and distributed networks like the

Few people had access to early mainframe computers like UNIVAC (pictured).

Internet, we now understand that the essential character of the computer is decentralizing.[30]

DECENTRALIZATION'S IMPACT ON SOCIETY

Decentralization is changing the balance of power in nearly all organizations. It affects the relationship between businesses and customers, mass media and their audiences, employers and workers, governments and the governed. No longer are corporate chief executive officers, media executives, and government officials the only ones who can quickly summon business, economic, and political data in a few keystrokes. Nor can they always withhold information from others. Now everyone—homemakers, workers, union organizers, students—has similar computing power at their fingertips. PCs have given individuals countless ways of bypassing those who in the past had almost exclusive control of information. For example, on-line investors now have direct access to market information about stocks and bonds and can conduct transactions themselves without relying on a stockbroker. Citizens can access and read government or historical documents for themselves instead of hearing them explained by opinion makers or journalists. Travelers can make airline reservations without the services of travel agents. People almost everywhere, even those in many nations under authoritarian rule, can communicate with thousands of others worldwide and avoid censorship.

Giving computing power to many people may be desirable in a country ruled by tyrants, but it could also produce troubles for a nation, including a democratic one. As author Esther Dyson observes, "[The Internet] undermines central authorities whether they are good or bad, and it helps dispersed forces to act together, whether *they* are good or bad."[31] This means that crusaders, dissenters, and even malcontents in many nations now have the ability to rapidly gather information, manipulate it to their own advantage, and send it across the Internet worldwide to sympathizers and supporters. Chinese university students, for example, were able to use computers to quickly inform their compatriots living abroad and others around the globe about a ruthless government crackdown on prodemocratic forces in the early 1990s. Within the United States, members of militia groups and racist groups regularly share on-line antigovernment views and sow the seeds of distrust of authorities. As new on-line communities such as these proliferate, they are marked by an odd phenomenon: none actually exists in the physical world. Instead, they all abide in a strange new world—cyberspace.

CYBER CULTURE

Before the arrival of the Internet, cyberspace did not exist. This realm did not even have a name until science fiction writer William Gibson created it in his 1984 novel, *The Necromancer*. Since then the term has gained worldwide acceptance as a way to define the domain where the events of the Internet appear to take place. For many, cyberspace is an electronic frontier where the natural world and the artificial world meet. Some observers refer to it as the interface between the world of the computers and the human mind.

Above all, it is a place where growing segments of humanity congregate and take part in what many call the "world's largest conversation." Here, people from all walks of life, from around the world, communicate, gather data, conduct business, transfer money, play games, commit crimes, harass

Thanks to the Internet, computer users can view information from all over the world without leaving the comforts of home.

and stalk others, take educational courses, seek companionship, organize political movements, and even worship God. From the privacy of their own homes, they can do this through the use of e-mail, newsgroups, and on-line chatrooms. Some users, who are otherwise lonely individuals, discover they have no trouble communicating with others in cyberspace. They develop enduring friendships on the Internet and now and then even fall in love and marry.

Some people spend an extraordinary number of waking hours working, socializing, and having fun on the Internet. Ex-

A young woman surfs the Internet at a cyber cafe.

plains Esther Dyson about her own life, "I live on the Net. It's the medium I use to communicate with many of my friends and colleagues. I also depend on it professionally: It's the primary subject about which I write, talk, and consult, and the basis of most companies I invest in, both in the United States and in Eastern Europe."[32]

Dyson is not alone. Growing numbers of individuals now spend hours every day before a computer monitor, logging on and off the Internet. Workdays spent at a PC are followed by evenings of communicating on-line with friends around the world, monitoring personal investments, and playing computer games. In the process, other forms of entertainment and community work have declined. Signs are strong that book reading, personal hobbies, volunteerism, and even television viewing have dwindled as more and more people explore the Internet. This shift in how people work and play has caused significant changes in how society functions. One of the biggest areas to experience change is the economy.

A Changing Economy

Although the Internet was never intended to be used for commercial purposes, it has nonetheless become an important new medium for economic activity. Around the clock, great portions of human work are digitally transmuted into millions of bursts of light that flash through fiber optic cables. Electronic versions of bank statements, résumés, work orders, construction bids, manuscripts, computer programs, blueprints, credit ratings, criminal records, and countless other documents flow constantly and almost instantaneously through computerized communication networks. In addition, growing numbers of individuals and organizations advertise, bid, buy, and sell their products and services online. They order parts, bill customers, make contracts, and carry out other types of commerce. Many even resolve business disputes with on-line mediators. Though the volume of sales on the Internet is still far less than that which is done by more convential means, the number of goods and services sold and bought on-line increases all the time. Vinton Cerf, one of the founders of the Internet, says, "I wouldn't be surprised if at least 15 or 20 percent, maybe 25 percent, of the world's economy is running on the Net by 2006."[33] If Cerf's estimate proves true, it would represent an estimated $8 trillion worth of economic activity.

More than just business transactions and advertising are taking place on-line. Many companies now also use the Internet as a powerful tool for recruiting talent. Conversely, a growing number of workers also use the Internet to obtain employment. Sociologist and business management expert Peter Drucker observes:

> The fastest-growing e-commerce in the United States is in an area where there was no "commerce" until now—in jobs for professionals and managers. Almost half of the world's largest companies now recruit through Web sites, and some two and a half million managerial and professional people (two thirds of them not even engineers or computer professionals) have their resumes on the Internet and solicit job offers over it. The result is a completely new labor market.[34]

THE ECONOMIC IMPORTANCE OF COMPUTER INFORMATION

By the end of the twentieth century, the flood of computer-based information had changed the economic structure of the world. In some countries information had become the basis of a new economy. No longer is agriculture the main source of employment for the peoples of North America and western Europe as it was in 1900. Nor is manufacturing the economic backbone in these same regions as was the case fifty years ago. New service-oriented industries now dominate the economy. Many of the new jobs are filled by knowledge workers who use computers to create, collect, store, send, manage, or sell information. A knowledge worker, according to Peter Drucker, is someone who applies the orderly arrangement of information to the world of work. And knowledge, he asserts, is now more important than land, raw material, or investment money as the basis for a modern economy.

Never before has information had such commercial value as it does in the Computer Revolution. Millions of people now base their business and financial decisions on the latest news about the stock market, farm prices, manufacturing, marketing, technology, banking, government, commerce, demographics, politics, climate, science, and many other topics. Business, government, and military leaders have learned that quick access to accurate data is essential to survival in an ever-globalizing world.

The economic importance of digital information is reflected in the rise of companies specializing in computer technology. The United States became the world's leading producer of computer software in recent years. As a result, huge software corporations such as Microsoft now possess economic power rivaling that of older manufacturing-based companies. As Microsoft founder Bill Gates points out, "The legacy of the [early phase of the Computer Revolution] is that 50 million PCs are sold each year worldwide, and that fortunes have been completely reordered in the computer industry."[35] Computers also play a significant role in the manufacturing industry. In recent years, the production of computers and telecommunications technology has become one of the nation's leading manufacturers.

The rise of the computer industry has also created a geographical shift in economic power in North America. Not long ago, older manufacturing cities, such as Cleveland and Detroit, were the nation's undisputed economic hubs. Today, however, areas such as Silicon Valley in California—the center of the American computer industry—have become the new economic power centers.

AN ALTERED WORKPLACE

Computer technology is also revolutionizing where most adults spend most of their waking hours: the workplace. Electric typewriters, filing cabinets, and adding machines made way for computers, printers, digital phones, scanners, and fax machines. Today, gleaming new office buildings are filled with rows of workers seated at computer workstations where they perform word processing, spreadsheeting, data entry, and information sharing with colleagues, clients, and suppliers around the world via the Internet.

Even the size and shape of some large buildings are being affected by the rise of electronic information. Efficient computers and telecommunication systems have reduced the need for great numbers of workers to congregate at a single, huge corporate skyscraper located in the downtown of a major city. Fewer workers gathering in a single location means companies can now build smaller buildings in cheaper areas outside of cities. This trend is evident in the fact that the Sears Towers, built in 1974, stands 417 meters high while Microsoft's headquarters in Redmond, Washington, is just 20 meters tall.

The Computer Revolution has also changed how many workers are organized and supervised. Throughout much of the twentieth century, large institutions used a hierarchal form of management. Generally, this meant that workers followed strict work rules and abided by a rigid chain of command when giving and carrying out instructions.

Today many of these management systems are gone. Instead, managers and supervisors have adopted workplace environments modeled after those in Silicon Valley. Under these new management systems, supervisors encourage teamwork, equality, informality, and flexible work hours.

Work has, in fact, become more transportable because of the Computer Revolution. Growing numbers of workers carry lightweight laptops or handheld computers wherever they travel. This allows them to do their work almost anywhere they can find modem connections. Some bypass these requirements by using PCs with wireless modems that beam data by radio signals. Because of these new gadgets, growing numbers of workers in the advanced nations do not even need to report to the traditional office anymore. Instead, these telecommuters do their work at home on PCs and send it where it is needed, any time, day or night.

Though most of these profound changes are taking place in wealthy, industrialized countries, many less advanced nations are also beginning to experience the economic impact of the computer. India, a nation with a half billion illiterate people, has become a leading producer of software. In Vietnam, where a software programmer makes just $200 a month, a small but growing industry exported $9 million worth of software in 1999. The Vietnamese government expects this figure to rise to $500 million by 2005.

Meanwhile, many other countries also recognize the importance computers play in the modern economy. Few want to be

PCs and modems have allowed increasing numbers of employees to work at home.

COMPUTERIZING THE ROUTINE THINGS OF LIFE

In his article, "Beyond the Information Revolution" in The Atlantic Monthly, social philosopher and author, Peter Drucker, explains what he believes the computer-based Information Revolution's biggest impact has been.

Like the Industrial Revolution two centuries ago, the Information Revolution so far—that is, since the first computers, in the mid-1940s—has only transformed processes that were here all along. In fact, the real impact of the Information Revolution has not been in the form of "information" at all. Almost none of the effects of information envisaged forty years ago have actually happened. For instance, there has been practically no change in the way major decisions are made in business or government. But the Information Revolution has routinized traditional *processes* in an untold number of areas.

The software for tuning a piano converts a process that traditionally took three hours into one that takes twenty minutes. There is software for payrolls, for inventory control, for delivery schedules, and for all the other routine processes of a business. Drawing the inside arrangements of a major building (heating, water supply, sewerage, and so on) such as a prison or a hospital formerly took, say, twenty-five highly skilled draftsmen up to fifty days; now there is a program that enables one draftsman to do the job in a couple of days, at a tiny fraction of the cost. There is software to help people do their tax returns and software that teaches hospital residents how to take out a gall bladder. The people who now speculate in the stock market online do exactly what their predecessors in the 1920s did while spending hours each day in a brokerage office. The processes have not been changed at all. They have been routinized, step by step, with a tremendous saving in time and, often, in cost.

left out, which is why many governments around the world now require computer training in their nation's schools.

IMPACT ON LEARNING

Because computers are indispensable in the modern workplace, education officials everywhere want to implement computers in their schools. Many educators and community leaders believe providing children with hands-on experience and familiarity with computers at an early age will help to produce productive future workers. To promote this concept, many companies donate computer equipment to schools and libraries.

Students in advanced countries now use computers at school for word processing and on-line research. Some schools rely on computers even more. Convinced that computers can also make learning easier, school districts everywhere have made huge investments in computers and educational software. These programs offer colorful video clips, lively sound, and music to interest and motivate students. Because of the computer's capacity to provide stimulating and often entertaining approaches to learning, many educators believe that in the near future the role of the teacher may be altered. Instead of lecturing and dispensing information, say some advocates of computer-based learning, teachers may instead become technology assistants who help students select appropriate software. Author Nicholas Negroponte believes computer simulation programs designed to imitate real life will offer students amazing new educational opportunities. He observes:

Until the computer, the technology for teaching was limited to audiovisual devices and distance learning by television, which simply amplified the activity of teachers and the passivity of children. . . . The computer changed this balance radically. All of a sudden, learning by doing became the rule rather than the exception. Since computer simulation of just about anything is now possible, one need not learn about a frog by dissecting it. Instead, children can be asked to design frogs, to build an animal with frog-like behavior, to modify that behavior, to simulate the muscles, to play with the frog.[36]

In addition to changing how students approach the content of various subjects, computers also expanded student access to distant educational resources. During the 1990s many secondary schools and universities began using computers for distance learning. This new approach to learning allows students to stay at home for part of the school day and do much of their work online. Students periodically visit their teachers for help and to take exams. Secondary

Most educators feel that computers are a valuable learning tool because they stimulate, involve, and often entertain the student.

schools generally provide a few on-line courses, but on the college level, some universities offer entire four-year and graduate degree programs.

Though the arrival of computers in schools has changed the way schools work and spend money on resources, many wonder if these changes are really beneficial. Some critics complain that school authorities often divert funds from other subjects, including shop, art, drama, or literature to buy computer technology. Some school officials have diverted spending on library books to buying computers instead. In Mansfield, Massachusetts, school officials a few years ago even cut teaching positions in music, art, and physical education and used that funding to spend $333,000 on computers. Similar budget decisions occur across North America every year. Author Clifford Stoll, a self-described "computer contrarian," thinks these priorities are wrong. He argues:

> Throngs of educators, lemming-like, line up to wire their schools. Parents grin as they plunk down credit cards to buy electronic machines for their children, anticipating their kids getting a jump start or a quick fix. Meanwhile, English teachers must deal with the cry for computer literacy while coping with semi-literate students itching to play with computers who can't read a book.[37]

THE GREAT DIGITAL DIVIDE

As schools search for ways to make the best use of computers, a serious digital divide between those with and those without computer skills is taking shape. Income levels partly explain the disparity. According to a 1999 U.S. Department of Commerce study, 80 percent of American households earning $75,000 a year have computers, but only 16 percent of households making $10,000 to $15,000 own them.

But race also appears to be a factor. According to a 1999 U.S. Department of Commerce study, 47 percent of white households have computers, but only 23 percent of African Americans and 26 percent of Hispanics own them. Asian Americans, meanwhile, are far more likely than any other racial group in the United States to own computers.

The study also indicates that low-income whites are also twice as likely to have a computer as blacks on the same economic level. Some scholars suspect that cultural differences help explain why many African Americans are reluctant to embrace computers. They believe many black youth, especially those of the inner cities, view computers as play things of "nerdy" white boys. Others, including Harvard professor of humanities Henry Louis Gates Jr., think the problem is more complicated. Lack of professional role models, lingering feelings of social and cultural isolation, and lack of initiative may also play a role, he argues. Gates warns that African Americans must embrace the new technology or face the possibility of being left behind in the new computer-based economy:

> Make no mistake about it: Unless we utilize the new information technology to build and deepen the form of social connection, slavery, a century of segregation, and subsequent class divisions within the black community have severed,

One study shows that only 23 percent of African Americans own computers, prompting the view of some analysts that a type of "cyber segregation" is developing.

African Americans will face a form of cyber-segregation in the coming century just as devastating to the aspirations of the black community in its way as Jim Crow segregation was to our ancestors. But this time, the fault will be our own.[38]

Other observers agree with Gates that African Americans may suffer economic, social, and political setbacks if they fail to keep pace with other races in learning computer technology. Writes Frederick L. McKissack Jr., a Web designer and freelance writer, "I am one of the few African Americans in this country who has a computer at home, uses one at work, and can use a lot of different kinds of software on multiple platforms. According to those in the know, I'm going to remain part of that very small group for quite some time."[39]

The United States is not the only nation to experience the digital divide. The problem is also international. The divide underscores an important aspect of the Computer Revo-lution. Even though individuals around the world have PCs and communicate over the internet, most people on earth have no access to computer technologies whatsoever. For the most part, the poor nations are the ones that are the least able to participate in the Computer Revolution. As a result, these countries often find the gap between themselves and the advanced nations widening. National leaders everywhere now realize that a mastery of computer technology bestows upon any society political, military, and economic advantages. Those left behind by the Computer Revolution may one day soon find themselves poorer and lacking power. "Today's computer technology is rapidly turning us into three completely new races: the super poor, the rich, and the super rich,"[40] says Gregory Rawlins, author of *Moths to the Flame: The Seductions of Computer Technology.* Unlike the advanced nations of North America, Europe, and elsewhere, most of the world plays no role in

HORROR FOR SALE IN CYBERSPACE

In this abbreviated version of his essay in Time *magazine, Stephen King, the best-selling author of horror stories, relates his impressions of electronically publishing a novel on the Internet. Though this particular on-line project was later suspended, King later became involved in other Internet-publishing endeavors.*

In July of this year [2000], I began publishing a serial novel at my website, stephenking.com. The idea was one episode a month, pay as you go . . . and pay by the honor system. My inspiration was the newspaper vendors in New York City during the first half of the century. Many of those hired for the job were blind, because the distribs felt that even slightly dishonest people wouldn't steal from a blind newsboy. . . .

Am I displeased with how things have turned out? Nope. I've had terrific fun working on *The Plant*, and so far it's grossed about $600,000. It may end up over a million (the figures will be posted on the website early next year, down to the last crying dime). Those aren't huge numbers in today's book market, but *The Plant*—pay attention, now, because this is the important part—is not a book. Right now it exists as nothing but electronic bits and bytes dancing gaily in cyberspace. Yes, it's been downloaded by hundreds of thousands of people, either in its various parts or in its entirety, and some readers may have printed hard copies (even decorated them like medieval monks illuminating manuscripts, for all I know), but mostly it's just an electronic mirage floating out there all by itself . . . with no printing costs, publisher's cuts or agent's fees to pull it down. Advertising aside (I did some, not much), costs are low to the point of nonexistence, and the profit potential is unlimited.

the Computer Revolution. In fact, only 5 percent of the world's population used the Internet in 2000.

Lack of resources prevent technological progress in many other poor nations where people lack basic infrastructure components such as highways, sewage systems, and telephone lines. In 2001 the world had about 6 billion people, but only 500 million telephones—or one for every twelve people. In some underdeveloped countries, entire villages lack both telephones and telephone lines, thus making it impossible to connect to the Internet. The World Bank, a major international lending organization, has more telephones within its own organization than the entire country of Rwanda.

Without access to computers and the Internet, and without the ability to use and understand them, a nation cannot compete with those that have these resources and skills. How to respond to these problems and other challenges unleashed by the Computer Revolution vexes world leaders everywhere.

Chapter

5 Challenges to Society

Even as various nations acquire the skills and technology needed to join the Computer Revolution, they face new trials and challenges. Foremost among them are questions of universal service. Should computer technology be available only to those who can afford it? Or, should government resources be used to ensure that all within a society, rich and poor alike, have access?

This is not the first time governments have grappled with such issues. In the past, governments everywhere wrestled with the question of universal postal service. Today, most governments guarantee that mail carriers will deliver mail to even the most remote residences, even when it is not cost effective. Increased postal charges or taxes usually provide the funds for making these deliveries possible. Universal telephone service is also common in some nations. Telephone subscribers often pay slightly higher charges to ensure that everyone is connected.

Now the argument has shifted to the Internet. To address the problem in the United States, Congress passed the Telecommunications Competition and Deregulation Act in February 1996. Though the law requires telephone, cable, and satellite communication companies to provide low-cost Internet access to schools, clinics, and hospitals, it does not guarantee true universal access.

Many political leaders want the government to do more. They propose that the federal government provide subsidies to telecommunication companies to make universal service a reality. Some consumer advocates think these corporations should be

Al Gore looks on as Bill Clinton signs the Telecommunications Competition and Deregulation Act.

As technology expands, computers and their users require more effective ways to manage the overwhelming amount of information.

required to provide public pay Internet stations, similar to pay telephones. Others, however, are wary of government intrusion. Instead, they want the Internet Service Provider companies to continue competing for customers, just as other companies would.

As policy makers try to respond to the question of computer access, they must also address other new issues. Among them is how to cope with a growing flood of information.

Coping with an Information Overload

Four hundred years ago, with the invention of the movable-type printing press, the number of available books began to double every seven years. Today the world is experiencing the same growth rate in the production of technical, scientific, and business documents. An estimated 5 million electronic databases now exist worldwide. At least 2 billion websites may now be on the Internet. These sources, plus growing amounts of data flowing from CD-ROMs, television, radio, books, periodicals, and various forms of mass communications, continue to produce a staggering amount of information that is unparalleled in history.

To keep up with the growing glut of data, engineers have developed automated computer systems that categorize, sort, analyze, store, retrieve, and transport enormous amounts of information at near-lightning speed. Electronic storage, however, presents problems. Information specialists must decide what data is worth saving because computer memory space is often limited. Another problem is that all too often, many institutions big and small discover that earlier computer models and software once used to save important data are incompatible with newer, upgraded technologies. As years roll by and employees change, old passwords and codes are lost or forgotten. Given enough time new workers often either overlook or have no knowledge of what information previous office workers set aside many years before.

SECURITY CONCERNS

While some information managers struggle to preserve data, others try to protect it from being copied, stolen, destroyed, or altered. How to keep information secure is fast becoming one of the biggest challenges of the Computer Revolution. The electronic form makes computer data especially vulnerable. Employees of the Central Intelligence Agency (CIA) and other government institutions that work with classified and secret information fear that spies who gain access to government computer files can easily copy them, store them in devices as small as wristwatches, and smuggle them past security systems.

This danger became apparent in the spring of 2000 when federal government officials learned that the head of the CIA illegally downloaded sensitive information and took it home to read on his personal computer. Though no state secrets were lost, the fact that anyone could have done this so easily underscores the vulnerability of computer secrets.

When computers connect to the Internet, they become even more vulnerable. As writer Robert X. Cringely points out, "Despite the fact that the ARPAnet was developed originally to carry data between defense contractors, there was never any provision made for data security. There simply is no security built into the Internet."[41]

That lack of security continues into the twenty-first century. Among those eager to exploit this vulnerability are online vandals known as hackers. These individuals exist all over the world and use their computer prowess to hack into—or gain entry into—other computers. Some of these intruders are self-proclaimed cyber punks, who proudly consider themselves the Internet's bad boys. Some cyber punks are pranksters who derive personal pleasure from using their on-line computer skills to break security codes set up to protect computers belonging to commercial banks, governments, military installations, and other institutions. For the most part, these hackers are content to merely demonstrate how clever they are without getting caught. Other hackers are malicious. They alter, disrupt, and destroy files and programs. Some release computer viruses—special computer programs designed to ruin files and software indiscriminately—to infect computers. Sometimes hackers manage to steal by breaking into the computer files and manipulating financial accounts to their own advantage.

Throughout the year 2000, hackers periodically took over 155 computers belonging to 32 federal agencies, according to a study conducted by the U.S. Health Care Financing Administration, which controls Medicare.

About 75 percent of these attacks came from foreign soil. "I think it would come as quite a surprise for most Americans to learn the extent to which these federal civilian agencies are the target of attacks by foreign and domestic sources bent on espionage or other malicious attacks,"[42] says Rep. Billy Tauzin, a Republican congressman from Louisiana.

But hackers and cyber punks are the not the only ones penetrating the privacy of computer users. Cyber spies are also at work.

THREATS TO PRIVACY

Because hundreds of millions of computers are connected to the Internet and other networks, they are always vulnerable to some sort of on-line cyber surveillance being conducted by various individuals, organizations, and groups who are also connected. As Gregory Rawlins notes, "Now that electronic information about everyone and everything is publicly available, surveillance has branched out from its ancient roots in spying and become the province of big business, organized crime, and every computer-literate person."[43] For whatever reason it is being done, cyber surveillance means that millions of human beings worldwide are experiencing an ever-accelerating loss of personal privacy. How to handle this phenomenon worries government officials everywhere.

Almost everyone on the Internet today is exposed to on-line surveillance. This lack of privacy was not always the case. During the early days of the Internet, user anonymity was the rule. But as on-line business transactions and government services multiplied, the need to keep accurate records of on-line transactions also increased. To address this concern, the Intel Corporation put into its Pentium III processors hard-coded serial numbers that were supposed to enable the company to track and monitor its customers as they navigated the Internet. Microsoft

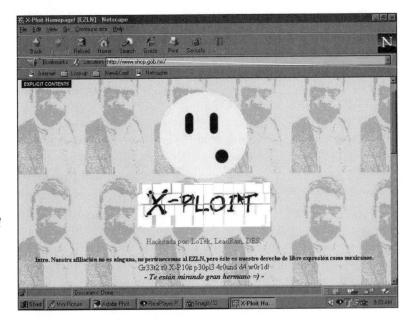

Mexico's Finance Ministry home page after hackers defaced it with anti-government propaganda. Government computers are particularly attractive targets for many hackers.

also got involved. It produced a code called Globally Unique Identifiers (GUID) that marked files and gave others a way of identifying who was responsible for creating those files. Though Microsoft claims GUIDs were originally intended to help retrieve lost work on the Internet, its GUIDs, along with other tracing software, now provide powerful tools for on-line trackers.

Another widely used tracking device is called a cookie. Maryanne Murry Buechner of *Time Digital* explains how cookies work:

> A cookie is a short string of data used to identify you, the Web user, to the Website that put it there. It allows the site to recognize you every time you visit and to trace your activity—particularly which pages you pull up. (That's invaluable information for the site's advertisers.) Once it identifies you, a site may also call up other personal information stored in its database: topics you've shown an interest in, the last books you bought from that site, maybe even your name and E-mail address—but only if you willingly revealed those details when first asked.[44]

These on-line tracking devices are of great value to marketing firms. By keeping records of the Internet visits of millions of people on-line, these firms hope to discover individual shopping habits, interests, tastes, preferences, and any number of other useful facts that they can sell to other businesses, marketers, advertisers, creditors, and political parties.

Businesses are not the only ones to track website visitors. A congressional report released in April 2001 found that sixty-four websites of the U.S. government use devices that enable various agencies to track the Internet behavior of website visitors, despite federal restrictions against the practice. Tracking is officially allowed only when the government believes there is a compelling need and agency officials have approved the procedure, and even then, federal law requires the government to inform Internet users that they are being tracked after visiting a government website.

OTHER COMPUTERIZED SOURCES

On-line surveillance is only one way governments, organizations, and businesses gather valuable data. Information gatherers also use on-line surveys, public records, magazine subscriptions, warranty information, credit ratings, and many other facts stored in computer databases. More than 5 billion computerized records exist in the United States alone that contain personal information about individuals. Many of these records are maintained by government agencies. The federal government of the United States supports at least 2,000 data banks for 178 of its biggest agencies and departments. Many of these files contain data about births, social security numbers, family members, salaries, tax information, employment histories, credit ratings, mortgage payments, legal transactions, criminal records, and many other facts. Commercial organizations also maintain huge data banks. Today, companies such as TRW, Equifax, and Trans Union specialize in gathering, maintaining, selling, and trading computerized files on more than 160 million people.

Because this information has high market value, some individuals are willing to break the law to get the data when it is not always available to the public. Computer-savvy criminals, for instance, break into the electronic files of government agencies, banks, businesses, and the military to steal information. In addition, some employees at huge institutions download data from the computers at their workplace and sell it to a number of eager customers. Notes writer Peter F. Eder of *The Futurist* magazine:

> Buyers of this material include insurers, lawyers, employers, private detectives, and bill collectors. Investigators say the biggest trading is with lawyers seeking information about litigants, health-care operations wanting data about people trying to collect claims, and employers doing background checks on prospective employees.
>
> Typically, thieves bribe Social Security workers for files that can then be sold for as much as ten times the price of the bribe.[45]

THE PRICE OF PRIVACY LOSS

Every day vast amounts of private information on millions of people—without their knowledge or permission—is gathered, sorted, analyzed, sold, traded, and saved by powerful computers. Even when individuals are aware that they are being tracked, they may lack the computer skills to stop the practice.

Many people believe this loss of privacy is simply the cost of taking part in a new and still largely unregulated communication medium. Others disagree and seek ways to keep communications on the Internet private. One way to ensure privacy is to use software that encrypts, or encodes, computer messages such as e-mail, before they are sent across the World Wide Web. Recipients of these messages unlock them with another software program known as a key.

Encryption software, however, is controversial. The U.S. government forbids the exporting of encryption software because it fears the product could become a powerful tool in the hands of terrorists and other enemies of the nation.

U.S. attorney general Janet Reno testifies at a congressional committee hearing on encryption in 1999.

Are Computers a Good Idea for Students?

In her book, Failure to Connect: How Computers Affect Our Children's Minds—for Better and Worse, *Jane M. Healy, Ph.D., questions the suggestion that computers in the classroom will improve learning.*

Technology shapes the growing mind. The younger the mind, the more malleable it is. The younger the technology, the more unproven it is. We enthusiastically expose our youngsters to new digital teachers and playmates, but we also express concern about the development of their brains, bodies, and spirits. Shouldn't we consider carefully the potential—and irrevocable—effects of this new electronic interface with childhood?

Today's children are the subjects of a vast and optimistic experiment. It is well financed and enthusiastically supported by major corporations, the public at large, and government officials around the world. If it is successful, our youngsters' minds and lives will be enriched, society will benefit, and education will be permanently changed for the better. But there is no proof—or even convincing evidence—that it will work.

The experiment, of course, involves getting kids "on computer" at schools and at home in hopes that technology will improve the quality of learning and prepare our young for the future. But will it? Are the new technologies a magic bullet aimed straight at success and power? Or are we simply grasping at a technocentric "quick fix" for a multitude of problems we have failed to address?

Such a problem already exists within the United States. Criminals often use encryption to conceal their illicit on-line activities from law enforcement officials. As a countermeasure, various government agencies want the legal right to use software that allows them to read suspicious on-line transmissions. James Kallstrom, a former FBI official, argues that giving law enforcement agents this power is in keeping with current practices: "Law enforcement today violates individual privacy all the time, but it's done under court order. This [use of encryption software] is no different from wiretapping a phone. People do have a right to privacy; we want privacy for innocent people, commerce and business. But if the parties violate the law, they give up that right."[46]

Many civil libertarians, however, fear that law enforcement officers could also use encryption software to intrude into the private communications of law-abiding citizens. They also argue that giving governments the ability to pry into personal correspondence is an affront to American values. As Simson Garfinkel, a fellow at the Berman Center for Internet and Society at Harvard Law School, observes:

> Today, technology is killing one of our most cherished freedoms. Whether you call this freedom the right to digital self-determination, the right to informational autonomy [independence] or simply the right to privacy, the shape of our future will be determined in large part by how we understand, and ultimately how we control or regulate, the threats to this freedom that we face today.[47]

As lawmakers grapple with the encryption issues, another battle is under way over an issue that has bedeviled societies and governments for centuries.

NEW DEBATES OVER CENSORSHIP

What information should be available to the people of any community? Who should have access to this information? And who shall decide these matters? Such questions have always been difficult for any society to resolve, but they are especially troublesome in the age of the Internet. Unlike other media such as television and radio, no central authority exists on the Internet that governs or monitors most of the information flow. For the most part, the Internet resembles an international highway with no border guards, police, or highway patrol cars. With some exceptions, people are free to go wherever they please. They can also distribute and gather almost any type of material imaginable.

Some users like this anarchic quality and oppose any government control. Cyber punks are especially animated on this topic. Many have vowed to do whatever they must to protect their privacy and freedom on-line and to roam the Internet anonymously, answerable to no one.

However, not everyone is certain that unbridled access to the Internet is good. Critics worry about the steady rise of websites featuring pornography, propaganda, screeds of hate from racist groups, plans for making illegal weapons, and many other dangerous and antisocial material. They argue that restrictions are needed at least to protect young children from pedophiles, stalkers, and unscrupulous advertisers. One proposal is to mandate the use of filter software in public schools and libraries to prevent certain offensive material from being accessed. Senator John McCain of Arizona favors the use of filters and argues, "All schools and libraries should have the capability to filter out this offensive material. And if we are using taxpayers' dollars to pay for their Internet access . . . then I believe these institutions also have an obligation to act to restrict this type of material."[48]

Anticensorship groups, however, are wary. They claim filters do not always work as intended. For instance, a filter may respond to a keyword—such as sex—and prevent computer access not only to pornographic websites, but also others featuring biology, health, and anatomy. Many of these critics also argue that computer filters in public libraries interfere with the lawful access of information by adult patrons. Barbara Ford, the 1997–98 president of the American Library Association, approves of parental use of filters on home PCs. But she opposes them in public libraries: "We think the best way to protect children is to teach them to use technology and make good choices, not put blinders on. It is imperative for students of all ages to learn critical-viewing and information skills that will help them make good judgments about the information they encounter." [49]

Censorship is only one of the issues raised by the use of filters. Tracking of school children is another. In September 2000, N2H2, Inc., a Web filter company, and the Roper Starch Worldwide marketing firm, combined forces to put child-tracking files in classroom computers. Many schools use N2H2's filter to keep out offensive material, but in so doing they allow the company to track students' Web-browsing habits. The company then sells monthly reports of the data it collects to large corporations such as Big Chalk, Inc. The U.S. Department of Defense, hoping to refine its recruitment of older teens into the armed forces, is another customer. Gary Ruskin, director of Commercial Alert, a network dedicated to protecting children from commercial exploitation, is critical of the plan. He argues, "Is this what the public schools and the compulsory schooling laws are for? Is this something that teachers feel proud of—to preside over a corporate market research factory that touts its [capability

A young girl plays games on the Internet at a public library. Many libraries grapple with the question of whether they should offer uncensored Internet access.

CLARIFYING THE DEBATE

In his article "It's Time to Tackle Cyberporn" published in Taking Sides: Clashing Views on Controversial Issues in Science, Technology, and Society, *by McGraw-Hill/Dushkin, British writer John Carr argues that some sort of censorship is not only needed, but inevitable.*

The Great Internet Freedom Debate is rolling forward. At issue is the balance to be struck between "free speech" and the ability of families, employers, schools or other organizations to protect themselves against the receipt of material that is unwanted, illegal or both. The responsibility for striking the balance—and providing mechanisms to enforce it—is, however, increasingly seen not as a job for governments, legislatures or police forces, but for private citizens and the private companies that own and run the Internet industry.

There is a tenacious cyber-myth that the Internet is a vast, anarchic forum, beyond the reach of any government or authority, uncontrolled and uncontrollable. The reality is that for all parts of the Internet there are several potential points of control. . . . So this debate is not about whether some sacred principle of non-regulation or freedom from censorship should be breached: that point was passed some time ago. Now we are discussing practical questions of degree: the ways in which intervention or regulation might occur; the level at which a censorship option might be feasible or appropriate.

If you link up to the Internet with the big UK [United Kingdom]-based Internet service providers (ISPs), such as AOL, MSN, Compuserve, Poptel or LineOne, you already do not enjoy full and unrestricted access to the superhighway. . . . Most of what is kept from you is illegal material, principally child pornography. . . .

The Internet is far from a stable or mature technology. . . . It serves no one's interest to pretend we are on the brink of some last-ditch defence of democracy and free speech when we engage in this debate. Instead we should all recognize that almost all of us are looking, in good faith, for new answers to the new problems thrown up by the new technology.

to penetrate the minds] . . . of the children entrusted to them?"[50]

So far, all attempts to impose regulation of controversial data on-line have met stiff resistance from many free-speech advocates. American courts have also balked at attempts to introduce censorship on the Internet. In 1996, for example, Congress passed the Communication Decency Act, designed to curtail access to on-line pornography. But the U.S. Supreme Court later struck down the law as a violation of protected free speech.

Attempts to convince ISPs to impose restrictions on the access of controversial material have had more success, though not without controversy. In recent years, the governments of Germany and France have pressured various ISPs operating in those countries to block access to on-line material from Nazi and child pornography websites.

Even if ISPs agree to block certain materials, chances are their efforts will be in vain. Many industry analysts doubt these companies or any other organizations could ever possibly monitor the vast stream of data flowing over the ever-expanding Internet. Writes *Newsweek*'s Steven Levy, "Requiring network providers to monitor what goes out over their systems is unworkable—it's like asking the phone companies to monitor what's uttered in billions of conversations. The only way that you can really control content is to cripple the whole network."[51] Even when filters are in use, resourceful Internet users almost always find other ways to access material.

As communities around the globe grapple with these questions of censorship, they also must contend with a growing number of unique legal questions arising from the Computer Revolution.

LEGAL PROBLEMS

Before the arrival of the Internet, various companies and businesses throughout the world have used similar, or even identical, logos, trademarks, and company names, without ever becoming aware of one another. But in the age of the Internet this is no longer the case. Today, as the Internet grows internationally, various owners of websites are becoming more proprietary about their business images. Consequently, many have gone to court, seeking clarification over who has the legal right to a particular corporate name, initials, or logo.

On-line defamation is another growing problem. Many websites now exist for the sole purpose of discrediting or attacking a particular person, organization, company, group, or product. Angry customers have also used the Internet to lambaste a company or individual they believed has treated them unfairly. Among the most controversial websites are those that advocate or condone murder. In 1998 gynecologist Dr. Barnett Slepian was murdered near Buffalo, New York. Soon afterward his name appeared on an antiabortion website, crossed off a list of abortion doctors in North America. The website also contained pictures of dripping blood and the names, addresses, and websites of dozens of physicians, clinic workers, and prochoice celebrities. In addition, the website categorized these doctors in three ways: whether they were still "working," "wounded," or had become a "fatality." Law enforcement officials have been exploring whether such websites illegally encourage acts of violence.

Because of growing legal disputes, many law firms now specialize in Internet cases. But taking legal action over what happens in cyberspace is not a simple matter. For one thing, national and political boundaries do not exist in cyberspace. Nor is it clear which law enforcement agencies and courts have jurisdiction when a wrongful action or civil dispute on-line occurs. For example, insurance companies doing business under government guidelines in one particular geographical area or country may encounter legal problems if they use the Internet to sell insurance on-line in areas that forbid these services. Sending Nazi literature on the Internet may be illegal in Germany, but it is permissible in the United States. Debates arise over who has jurisdiction when, for example, an American sends on-line Nazi material into Germany. The nation where the on-line action was sent? Or the nation where the action was received? So far, no clear answers to these kinds of questions have arisen.

Questions of decency are also emerging. Images considered pornographic in one country may be considered within the limits of decency in another. There are also debates over what constitutes fair advertising. Advertisements that compare one product unfavorably with another is acceptable in the United States, but it violates the law in other countries.

Among the most contentious of all on-line legal disputes is that of copyright protection. Before the Computer Revolution most U.S. copyright laws were clear: Use of copyrighted material belonging to authors, musicians, artists, filmmakers, and other creative people without their permission was prohibited.

However, the arrival of digital technology and the unregulated information flow on the Internet now makes it hard, if not impossible, to enforce these laws. New computerized equipment provides an easy way for almost anyone to digitize any written document, photograph, film, or musical recording and convert it into a computer file that can be easily sent across the Internet.

MUSIC COPYRIGHT DISPUTES

One of the most celebrated cases over copyright infringement involves Shawn Fanning, who, as a nineteen-year-old American college dropout, developed software that allowed him to send computer files to his friends over the Internet of musical recordings he had downloaded from CDs onto his PC. Later, Fanning developed his system into Napster, a successful on-line business, which allowed anyone on the Internet to download songs from the computers of others connected to the Internet. Though Napster initially charged nothing for this service, it did make money through advertising and other services.

Napster's actions, however, caused big problems. University Internet sources were tied up for hours while students obtained free music. This, plus fears that Napster may have been violating copyright laws, prompted two hundred universities and colleges to ban access to Napster on campus.

Many recording companies and artists were also unhappy. Convinced that Napster was both violating U.S. copyright laws and costing the industry and artists billions of dollars worth of sales and royalties, five large U.S. record companies sued to shut the company down.

In court, Napster's defenders argued that the new technology makes old copyright laws unenforceable. Fanning's attorneys

Shawn Fanning, creator of Napster, an on-line business that allowed Internet users to download music from other computers.

claimed the recording industry now has no choice but to reconsider how it distributes music and charges customers for its products. Nonetheless, in February 2001, a federal appeals court panel ruled that Napster's 50 million users violated copyright laws every time they exchanged songs without permission. The company was told to cease operations.

Though the record industry was pleased with the court ruling, the practice pioneered by Fanning is far from disappearing. Napster and other similar companies are searching for equitable ways to charge a fee for their services, which will help pay copyright costs. Some industry observers predict that other on-line song-swapping companies can easily relocate outside of the United States and continue their operations in cyberspace without fearing lawsuits filed in American courts.

As the Internet expands, legal cases such as Napster will most likely increase as well. Internet pioneer Vinton Cerf points out:

A whole raft of policy issues that the Internet is facing needs attention. In which jurisdiction do we resolve a dispute concerning an electronic transaction? There are questions about privacy and confidentiality questions about the use of cryptography. Gosh, the list goes on and on. Policy issues the Internet raises are at least as important, maybe more important, than the hardware problems or the basic technology problems.[52]

Finding solutions to these challenges will be difficult because the Computer Revolution shows no sign of slowing down. Among the toughest to address are those that reflect the dark side of the Computer Revolution.

6 The Dark Side of the Computer Revolution

Almost all new technologies have proven to be both a blessing and a curse to humanity. The automobile, for instance, revolutionized transportation, but it also causes millions of highway deaths. Pesticides boost agricultural output, but they also damage wildlife and ecosystems. The paradox of nuclear power technology is that it makes possible both electricity and hydrogen bombs.

Computer technology is no different. Despite its bounty of benefits to humanity, it, too, has a dark side. As author Esther Dyson observes, "The Net gives awesome power to individuals—the ability to be heard across the world, the ability to find information about almost anything . . . along with the ability to spread lies worldwide, to discover secrets about friends or strangers, and to find potential victims of fraud, child abuse, or other harassment."[53]

EMPOWERING SOCIETY'S DEPRESSED AND DEPRAVED

The mentally disturbed, the malcontent, the evil, and the depraved have populated all societies. Until recently, however, such individuals seldom sought their twisted pleasures in public. Instead, most lurked in society's shadows.

The Computer Revolution and the World Wide Web changed all that. Now even society's most despised individuals and groups have extraordinary new tools with which to extend their influence. On the vast and almost unregulated frontier of the Internet, the most hard core proponents of pornography, terrorism, murder, and hate can promote their own causes and goals without much fear of being apprehended. On-line censors are few. Detection of wrongdoers is difficult. Laws are difficult to enforce in cyberspace.

The Internet has provided a new forum for those who hate. Websites abound for groups such as the Ku Klux Klan, neo-Nazi organizations, and others who express a violent hatred toward certain racial and ethnic groups. Hate also spurs the beliefs of many anarchists and antigovernment groups bent on the destruction of state authority. These groups and individuals provide more than just angry words on their websites. On-line visitors can also find tips on how to inflict death, destruction, and mayhem upon society, including do-it-yourself bomb-making plans and free software for creating computer viruses. Although such material existed before the Computer Revolution, never before has it been so accessible to millions of people in the privacy of their own homes.

Another dark side of the Internet involves suicide. South Korea, where use of the Internet is exploding, has thirty websites on suicide. They range from those that offer counseling and prevention to others that advocate suicide, including tips on how to commit suicide and advertise for suicide partners. In the spring of 2001, Koreans were shocked to learn that a young man was so depressed that he allegedly hired a nineteen-year-old from the Internet to kill him for $910.

The dark side of the computer revolution has also brought about a proliferation of online obscenity and pornography. *Wired* magazine estimates that as many as 4 percent of the almost 2 billion websites are pornographic. Many of these feature material deemed degenerate and criminal by law enforcement even in countries with a strong tolerance of the depiction of sexual acts. Among the most depraved of these websites are those that depict children being tortured or raped.

The Internet has also proved to be a powerful new tool for sexual predators. In the past, predators stalked playgrounds and schools looking for children who would be used for sexual purposes. Now these individuals can troll the world looking for victims on the Internet. Predators often begin

A lawyer for the Anti-Defamation League, an organization that opposes anti-Semitism and bigotry, looks at a white supremacist website.

Although the Internet can entertain and educate children, it may expose them to dangers as well.

by the U.S. Congress, that reached the U.S. Supreme Court in 2001. The Free Speech Coalition, a group of businesses that sells sexually explicit material for an adult market, brought the case to court. The coalition's lawyer, H. Louis Sirkin, argues, "If you're not using a real minor, how can you have a crime? If it's a computer image and it's virtual reality, it's still not a real minor, it's not a child engaged in anything."[54] Government lawyers, however, argue that the 1996 act forbids the use of any image "that appears to be" or "conveys the impression" of a child involved in unlawful behavior. The fact that the image is computer-generated does not alter this fact, they say.

As American courts try to decide whether virtual child pornography is a punishable offense, other cyber stalkers are also prowling the World Wide Web. For the most part, these high-tech stalkers want to use the Internet to hurt somebody.

their pursuit by assuming a false name, striking up a conversation with a curious child in an Internet chatroom, and developing an on-line friendship. This relationship sometimes leads to a personal encounter between adult and child that ends in statutory rape, sodomy, or even murder.

Cyberspace adds an odd twist to the problem of on-line child pornography. Federal law in the United States forbids both featuring children in pornographic scenes and soliciting them to engage in such acts. But what if the images are not of real children and instead are computer-generated? This question was at the heart of a legal challenge to the Child Pornography Prevention Act, passed

CYBER STALKING

Cyber stalking is such a newly identified problem that America's legal system is still trying to figure out what behaviors constitute a crime. At this point, cyber stalking can be defined as an unwanted and unexpected communication over the Internet that frightens or distresses another person. For any number of reasons, cyber stalkers use computer technology to terrify, threaten, extort, and harass other people.

Like their child-predator counterparts, most cyber stalkers begin their pursuit by striking up an on-line conversation. Stalking behavior may take the form of flaming—

bombarding the victim electronically with verbal abuse or obscenities—or spamming—sending vast amounts of junk e-mail to overwhelm the victim's computer.

A cyber stalker sometimes threatens bodily harm. As reported by ABC News, for instance, in the spring of 2001, a North Hollywood, California, businessman received terrifying e-mail messages from an anonymous stranger. The first message threatened to bash his skull in. Another message assured the business man that failure to close down his thriving Internet business would be "the final nail in his coffin."[55] The message concluded, "I always win."[56]

When the man went to the police for help, he found there was little they could do. Tracking down cyber stalkers is difficult. Many are skilled enough to use computer technology to cover their trail. They often know, for instance, how to conceal their e-mail address by using various remailing services, bouncing messages around the world from one server to the next.

As cyber stalkers try to terrify their victims and evade law enforcement, other deviants are also busy using the Internet for their own purposes. They have one purpose in mind: crime.

CYBER CRIME

As the Internet becomes a medium for the transfer of billions of dollars, more criminals are using cyberspace as a forum for their crimes. Members of organized crime, extortionists, crooked salespersons, con artists, and a host of other criminals now routinely use the Internet to deceive, rob, defraud, and commit other crimes, such as hacking, financial fraud, and selling child pornography. Many cyber criminals also hack into

One dark side to the Internet is that users may fall victim to the growing amount of cyber crime.

business websites to steal funds, or to buy products on-line with stolen credit cards.

To many wrongdoers, the Internet represents an irresistible place to commit crimes. Unlike other acts of crime, those committed in cyberspace do not occur in a real physical place, making it difficult for authorities to investigate. Proving who was actually in command of a computer used in cyber crime is also hard to prove. Nor do cyber criminals need to be geographically close to their victims. Thanks to the Internet, they can commit theft thousands of miles from where they live. Because cyber criminals seldom encounter their victims in person, they often view their crimes as less serious than they really are.

Cyber crime is on the rise, perhaps doubling every year. According to the National Consumers League, Internet fraud complaints rose 600 percent between 1997 and 2000. British law enforcement estimates that 60 percent of Britain's on-line businesses have been hacked in recent years. A recent study by the Computer Society found that 70 percent of American companies were attacked by hackers.

Because so much of the world's wealth now flows in electronic form around the world, criminals find it easier than ever to hide their money in foreign bank accounts. Many wealthy Americans who cheat on their taxes find the Internet a godsend. By electronically sending their financial assets to banks in the Caribbean and elsewhere in the world, many of the affluent can conceal the value of their true wealth from the scrutiny of the federal government.

To keep pace with computer crime, many law enforcement agencies around the world have created special cyber or electronic crime units to track criminals and trace the flow of ill-gotten gains over the Internet. However, these units often lack the resources, training, and personnel to keep up with the rise in cyber crime. "I have a squad of ten special agents here in San Francisco," says Special Agent in Charge Bruce Gephardt, "and . . . every one will tell you that they're overworked and underpaid for the type of work they do."[57] Similar complaints are voiced across the United States.

JOB LOSSES

Computers also deprive many people out of money in a painful, yet legal way: by destroying well-paying jobs. Though computers have removed much of the drudgery, inaccuracy, and danger from the modern workplace, they have also cost many workers their jobs. Computers free employers from having to hire as many human workers as they once did.

Since the 1970s a growing number of businesses, companies, and government agencies have installed automated computerized systems to reduce the need for manpower. These systems, plus the desire of many companies to relocate their factories to countries with cheaper labor costs, have contributed to widespread losses of manufacturing jobs in industrialized countries.

Though manufacturing jobs were the first to disappear as a result of automation, many service jobs also vanished. "Between 1983 and 1993, American banks shed almost 180 thousand tellers—over a third of their work force,"[58] writes Gregory Rawlins. By 2001, U.S. corporations were laying off an estimated 2 million workers a year whose jobs were destroyed by automation. Though the economy absorbed most of these workers, many had to settle for lower paying work.

When computers made their debut in the workplace, many corporate executives and managers expected that only lower-level production workers would lose their jobs. But during the 1990s upper-level jobs disappeared, too, especially when companies used computerized artificial intelligence programs to streamline decision making and wring out waste. Eastman Kodak, the photographic equipment manufacturer, for instance, reduced its corporate management structure from thirteen management levels to four. "Just as the industrial revolution

ATMs, or automated teller machines, have eliminated thousands of bank teller jobs.

turned artisans into factory hands, the information revolution is turning white-collar workers into machine tenders,"[59] asserts Rawlins. Management consultant and best-selling author Tom Peters agrees, predicting that "90% of white collar jobs in the U.S. will be either destroyed or altered beyond recognition in the next 10 to 15 years."[60]

Signs are also strong that professional jobs could also be affected. Powerful new software programs already exist that can do much of the legal work performed by lawyers. Medical software is also available that makes diagnoses that are as good, if not better, than those made by physicians.

All these job losses are offset somewhat by a rise in new jobs associated with the computer industry. Computer engineering, programming, and technical assistance jobs are just some of the new jobs created by the Computer Revolution. But even high-tech jobs have vanished in recent years, and few of the vast numbers of those who lose their jobs to computerized automation are qualified for the positions that remain.

These problems are not confined to the advanced nations. Similar employment patterns are emerging worldwide. Many government officials worry that this trend could only add to the unemployment problems of a world that already has 850 million unemployed people and more workers swelling their ranks every day.

A Negative Impact on Physical and Mental Well Being

Another drawback of the computer is the negative impact it may have on the physical and mental well being of humans. Millions of people spend much, if not most, of their workday seated before computer monitors, typing repetitively up to eight hours or more every day. As a result, hundreds of thousands of workers have developed a crippling injury known as carpal tunnel syndrome—a malady that affects wrists, hands, and forearms and often requires corrective surgery. The sedentary work associated with computers also causes other physical problems such as obesity, back pain, and eye strain.

Ergonomic computer keyboards and office furniture designed to reduce or eliminate many of these ailments is now available. But investing in such equipment is expensive and therefore unpopular with many large companies and businesses. In response to their complaints, the U.S. Congress, with backing from President George W. Bush, withdrew legislation in March 2001 that health experts say would have protected 102 million workers from injuries caused by repetitive motions in the workplace.

Computers have also taken a toll on the mental health of many users. Among other things, computing has proven addictive for some. Some zealous computerists are so addicted to their PCs that they spend up to sev-

Ergonomic keyboards are designed to reduce strain on the hands, wrists, and arms of computer users.

ADDICTED TO INTERNET GAMES

In his book, High Tech Heretic: Why Computers Don't Belong in the Classroom and Other Reflections by a Computer Contrarian, *Clifford Stoll offers this interview that psychologist Kimberly Young had with a college student called "Steve," who spends sixty to seventy hours a week on-line playing Multi-User Dungeons Dimensions/Domains fantasy games, know as MUDs.*

MUDs are like a religion to me, and I'm a god there. I'm respected by all the other MUDders. . . . Even when I'm not playing, I wonder if there will be more newbies for me to kill that night or which other guys will be playing. I am in control of my character and my destiny in this world. My character is a legend and I identify with him . . . [although shy and ill at ease around women,] when I'm playing the MUDs, I'm not feeling lonely or mopey. I'm not thinking about my problems. . . . I want to stay on the MUDs as long as I possibly can.

enty hours a week online and neglect their own spouses, children, and friends.

Computing obsessions take many forms. Some PC addicts are obsessed with playing on-line games, or taking part in chatrooms, or merely surfing the Web for hours at a time. Others are hooked on websites that feature violence and pornography. Many become compulsive gamblers by playing games of chance offered by the hundreds of gambling sites on the Internet. As a result, many have squandered their family savings, gone into debt, and filed for bankruptcy, causing great anguish to their families and friends.

Though most computer users do not suffer from any form of computer addiction, many do feel overwhelmed by the growing flood of information and the rapidity of change caused by the Computer Revolution. Steven Levy of *Newsweek* describes the problem this way:

The revolution has only just begun, but already it's starting to overwhelm us. It's outstripping our capacity to cope, antiquating our laws, transforming our mores [ideas of right and wrong], reshuffling our economy, reordering our priorities, redefining our workplaces, putting our Constitution to the fire, shifting our concept of reality and making us sit for long periods in front of computer screens while CD-ROM drives grind out another video clip. [61]

The rapid obsolescence of computer hardware and software also fatigues many computers users. All too often, workers find that the new updated version of a software is not compatible with an earlier one, or that their PCs have insufficient memory to run the new system. Frustration runs high when users must regularly learn how to operate newer and usually more complicated software and hardware. Many wonder if all this extra work is worthwhile. Some studies suggest that computers may not really enhance productivity very much at all, when glitches, sabotage, retraining, incompatibility of software, and other aspects are considered.

IMPACT ON THE MIND

As adults struggle to keep up with the changing demands of computers at their workstations, they note that their children are the first generation ever to have grown up with these new machines. "The psychological impact of the Information Revolution, like that of the Industrial Revolution, has been enormous. It has perhaps been the greatest on the way in which young children learn,"[62] observes sociologist Peter Drucker.

Young people are generally more at ease with computers than their elders and have a power at their disposal no other children in history have had. But nobody really knows what impact computers have on the mental development of young people. Advocates of computer-based learning point out that interactive capabilities of computers, realistic simulations, and the availability of data on the Internet are invaluable educational tools that give young learners an edge over those lacking the resources.

But there is also the dark side. Critics of computer learning, including many educators, suspect that clicking a computer mouse or pushing a key to obtain instantaneous electronic data has made many young people intellectually lazy. These critics also claim that growing numbers of students unquestioningly accept whatever appears on the screen as valid information. In addition, some researchers believe computer learning actually hurts the intellectual development of young people. Colorful monitor displays, video clips, music, sound effects, and hyperlinks that allow computer users to skip from one computer file to another may be fun for children, but many educators suspect that these activities may actually hinder the development of critical thinking. Advocates of traditional learning also fear that if students abandon the printed page altogether, they may suffer intellectually. *Newsweek*'s Steven Levy asserts "there's a real danger in even a partial abandonment of narrative forms and rigorous modes of thought associated with logical arguments, where A leads to B. Multimedia's forte [strong point] is not reason, but hot emotional impact—the same ingredients that make local TV news compelling, yet less filling."[63]

Some psychologists suspect that computerized video games—the world's most popular application of computer software—contribute to violent behavior in children. Lieutenant Colonel David Grossman, a West Point psychologist, believes CD-ROM games like Doom desensitize children to violence and help condition some to become violent killers.

As troubling as these problems are, they are overshadowed by even more dangerous aspects of the dark side of the Computer Revolution. These problems represent a growing threat to all life.

DANGER TO LIFE

Although many advocates for the computer industry tout computers as a clean, efficient technology that will help preserve natural resources and make the world more environmentally safe, the opposite appears to be the case. Increasingly, people around the world are discovering that computers are responsible for major pollution problems. In fact, Ted Smith, executive director of the nonprofit Silicon Valley Toxic Coalition, argues "I can't think of anything in the household [except pesticides] that would present more of a problem than a computer."[64]

The manufacturing of hundreds of millions of computers produces vast amounts of pollution and toxic waste. Disposal of these machines is another growing problem. Because computers become outdated so quickly, their owners abandon them faster than they would other appliances such as televisions and radios.

Most PCs contain toxic substances such as lead, cadmium, mercury, chromium, and PVC plastics that eventually leach into water supplies when they are deposited in a landfill. When they are burned, they can also produce cancer-causing agents called carcinogens.

What to do about this growing problem baffles government officials. A study by Carnegie Mellon University suggests that by 2004, landfills in the United States will contain about 70 million obsolete computers. Authorities, however, doubt that the nation's

Some critics fear that too much computer use in education may impair students' critical thinking skills.

Computer equipment becomes outdated very quickly, creating a glut of old computers at disposal sites.

landfills will be able to handle so many discarded PCs because they are already at capacity now. Making matters worse, more discarded computers are on their way to the dump. According to a recent National Safety Council study, the United States will have almost 500 million outdated computers in need of disposal by 2007.

Some European governments are responding to the problem by requiring computer manufacturers to phase out the use of toxic elements in the production of PCs. They are also considering laws that would mandate the recycling of old computers, or require manufacturers to take back worn out products and detoxify them. Some industry

observers suggest the expense for such a massive undertaking should be built into the purchase price of a computer.

Experts say these practices could help reduce the ongoing damage, but they will not stop the pollution or the harm it poses to our ecology. As harmful as computer-based pollution is, however, it pales in comparison to another grave danger—one that has the potential for widespread killing.

COMPUTERS AS WEAPONS

Perhaps the most disturbing aspect of computers is their use in modern weaponry.

New technology changes the nature of war, and modern weapons are eliminating the need for human involvement in much of the fighting. Writer Gregory Rawlins notes, "In the 1940s, heavy bombers needed a crew of twelve; by the 1950s, that dropped to six; by the 1970s, it was four; and by the 1980s, only two. In the decades to come, there will be one, and then—like cruise missiles [which now exist] none."[65]

Removing humans from immediate fighting may seem desirable at first, but in the long run it may cost more lives. Serious students of war have long understood that the more distant warriors are from the actual fighting, the less horrified they are by the killing that occurs and the more willing that war should continue. The use of computerized weaponry may be eliminating the very human abhorrence to kill that is common to most combatants. As Richard Homes, author of *Act of War*, observes: "The development of new weapon systems enables the soldier, even on the battlefield, to fire more lethal weapons more accurately to longer ranges: his enemy is, increasingly, an anonymous figure encircled by a gunsight, glowing on a thermal imager, or shrouded in armour plate."[66]

New technology even transforms the "anonymous figure" into something less than human at all, thereby making the act of

Computers Don't Yet Think, They Computate

John R. Searles, the Mill Professor of the Philosophy of Mind at the University of California, Berkeley, dismisses the idea that computers can ever think as humans do, in this passage taken from a longer essay in Taking Sides: Clashing Views on Controversial Issues in Science, Technology, and Society, *published by McGraw-Hill/Dushkin.*

Years ago I gave a proof . . . [that shows that computers work with symbols, but biological brains have a consciousness that enables them to interpret and understand symbols, something computers can't do]—called the "Chinese room argument"—and the way it works is this: just imagine that you're the computer, and you're carrying out the steps in a [software] program for something you don't understand. I don't understand Chinese, so I imagine I'm locked in a room shuffling symbols according to a computer program, and I can give the right answers to the right questions in Chinese, but all the same, I don't understand Chinese. All I'm doing is shuffling symbols. And now, and this is the crucial point: if I don't understand Chinese on the basis of implementing the program for understanding Chinese, then neither does any other digital computer on that basis because no computer's got anything I don't have. It's the simplest argument in history, but you'd be surprised how many people have fits about it.

killing easier to do. Lieutenant Colonel Dave Grossman, author of *On Killing: The Psychological Cost of Learning to Kill in War and Society*, writes of an Israeli tank gunner who says that in modern war "you see it all as if it were happening on a TV screen. . . . It occurred to me at the time: I see someone running and I shoot at him, and he falls, and it all looks like something on TV. I don't see people, that's one good thing about it." [67]

As human beings elect to turn over battlefield decisions to computers, they become more vulnerable to machine error. Several times in recent years, malfunctioning computers falsely alerted U.S. Strategic Air Command of impending Soviet missile attacks.

In June 1980, for example, computers for the Strategic Air Command showed that two sea-launched ballistic missiles and Soviet intercontinental ballistic missiles had been fired and were headed toward the United States. In response, the U.S. military went on full alert, preparing to go to war. Fortunately, six minutes later, the alert was halted when engineers determined a faulty computer chip, and not a military attack, was responsible for the alarming images on American radar screens.

Another tragic incident of mistaken identity took place on July 4, 1988, when a U.S. warship in the Persian Gulf blew up an Iranian jetliner, killing 290 civilians. The Ameri-

Because computerized weapons such as cruise missiles (pictured) can be operated remotely, soldiers may become desensitized to the deaths these weapons inflict.

TIME SPEEDS UP

In his book High Tech, High Touch, *author John Naismith observes that the manner in which people experience time has changed in the Computer Revolution.*

The way we live in time has changed steadily in the last hundred years and drastically in the last ten. Our modern lives restrict our connection to nature's rhythms and sounds. A little more than a century ago, before electricity, cell phones, and e-mail, most Americans woke when the sun rose, went to bed when the sun set, ate home-grown meals, and worked close to home. People spoke of moments as fleeting, memories as lasting. . . . Days were based more on light than hours and years more on seasons than calendars. It took weeks for a letter to cross the country and more than that for a response.

Time was set by nature's rhythms: tides, lunar cycles, seasons, stars, sunrise, sunset, shadows, plants. . . .

In contrast . . . phrases today reveal a sense of urgency about time: lack of time, quick time, real time, face time, deadline, check list, multitask, behind, finding time, making time, losing time, filling time, killing time, spending time, wasting time, on time, out of time, time frame, fast-forward. . . .

More and more, what promises to save us time consumes our time. Consumer technology requires prioritizing needs, selecting brands, buying, installing, maintaining, upgrading.

can crew made no visual contact of the aircraft before firing. Instead, it relied on electronic monitoring equipment and wrongly concluded that the doomed airbus was an attacking Iranian F-14 fighter plane.

Nobody knows if computer technology will save or cost lives in the future. But what is certain is that the Computer Revolution is far from over, and computer mishaps are certain to recur.

7 An Unfolding Awesome Power

The transformations of human life already wrought by the Computer Revolution may be just the beginning. Current trends in technology portend even bigger changes in the near future. Among them are changes in computer technology. In the coming decades, fewer PCs and other computers may be linked to the Internet with telephone lines. Instead, many will connect by using radio-based signals. Growing numbers of machines will connect to cables that now bring television signals into households. Cable hookups allow PC users to utilize the new broad bandwidth technology, which enables data to be sent and received many times faster than it can travel via telephone lines. Computers may also soon be using power-line technology being pioneered by companies such as Florida-based Intellon. With this technology, computers use the A/C electrical wires found inside the walls of homes and buildings, instead of telephone wires or cables, as carriers for computer messages.

Computers will also continue to change in appearance. Becoming faster and more powerful, they may also shrink in size and become more easily transported. Some industry analysts expect that in the near future, many PC users will be doing all their personal computing on-line. This means the software programs they use, such as word processing and spreadsheeting, will be located in remote computers, and not in home computers. Users will also be able to save their work in on-line folders and files, which will allow access to their data on any computer anywhere.

The distinction between the typical home PC and other appliances may also shrink, as microchips are imbedded into a vast array of ordinary objects capable of interfacing with any other digital machine. MIT's Nicholas Negroponte, author of *Being Digital*, offers this prediction:

> Early in the [twenty-first century] your right and left cuff links or earrings may communicate with each other by low-orbiting satellites and have more computer power than your present PC. Your telephone won't ring indiscriminately; it will receive, sort, and perhaps respond to your incoming calls like a well-trained English butler. Mass media will be redefined by systems for transmitting and receiving personalized information and entertainment. Schools will change to become more like museums and playgrounds for children to assemble ideas and socialize

with other children all over the world. The digital planet will look and feel like the head of a pin.[68]

Attempts to bring about changes like those Negroponte envisions are already under way. Researchers at IBM, Xerox's Palo Alto Research Center (PARC), MIT's Media lab, and elsewhere are busy developing a wide array of devices imbedded with microchips that can connect to the Internet and other computerized systems. "The idea is nothing less than to make the world itself programmable,"[69] says Alan Daniel, a former researcher at Georgia Tech University.

New Chips

As demand for more computing power grows, engineers will continue to seek ways to make contemporary computers work more efficiently. But because silicon chips have certain physical limitations, engineers may have to turn to other computer technologies to meet the computing needs of the future.

The next generation of computers may not rely on the flow of electrons, as current PCs do. New light-based, or optical computers, may skip this process altogether and use laser-generated light beams instead. In an optical

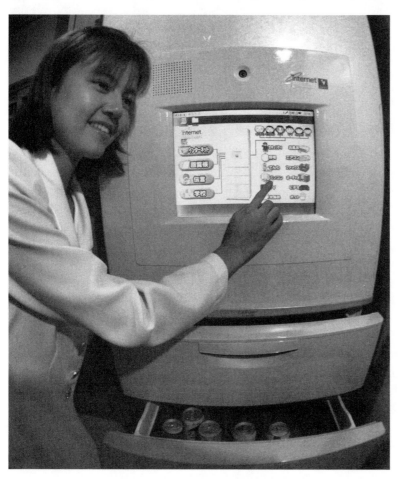

This Internet-linked refrigerator allows the user to access on-line recipes and suggested menus by touching the screen or speaking into the computer.

A prototype of an optical system. Optical computers use light beams instead of electricity to carry data.

computer, photons, or light particles, not electrons, carry data. In theory, optical computers offer many advantages. Because nothing travels faster than light, optical computers would be incredibly fast. Light waves also travel at different frequencies—which is why different colors exist. By using these different frequencies, optical computers could perform parallel computations—that is, simultaneous but different computer operations—rather than performing them sequentially, as most modern computers do. Bell Laboratories recently demonstrated an optical network that could carry 400 billion bits per second—an amount equivalent to all the data on the Internet—over a single fiber.

Researchers at IBM, Hewlett Packard, the Los Alamos National Laboratory, and elsewhere are working on another breed of machine: the quantum computer. Computing done in this type of computer takes place when either laser or radio beams are focused at spinning subatomic particles, which, in the strange world of quantum physics, can spin simultaneously in two directions. Quantum computers are designed to use this spinning phenomenon to perform computations at fantastic speeds.

Another candidate for the future is the molecular computer. The idea is to replace electron-based transistors found on microchips with a row of single molecules that electrochemically interconnect with each other in an interlocking chain. By controlling the opening and closing of these interconnections, the system creates logic gates needed for computing.

Research into biochemical computers is also under way. If this effort proves successful, computer engineers may one day replace silicon chips with a synthetic molecule of double-stranded DNA—the microscopic molecules found in the cells of all living organisms. These molecules contain the chemical instructions for replicating life by varying sequences of four chemical bases, symbolized by the letters A, C, T, and G. In humans, these sequences provide the chemical code that instructs cells how to produce features such as eye color, hair texture, the shape of an earlobe, the sex of an individual, and all the other characteristics of a human being.

The current use of the binary system (based on the digits 1 and 0, which provides the on-and-off switching method that controls the flow of electricity in modern computers) may also change. DNA-based computers offer even greater computer potency. When the A, C, T, and G chemical bases are used multiple times in alternating sequences to make very long sequences hundreds of letters long, the possibilities for different codes runs into the trillions. This gives a DNA computer vast memory storage power. As John S. MacNeil of *U.S. News & World Report* explains, "Because of DNA's power to store information—a few grams of the material could store all the data known to exist in the world—some scientists believe that such biochemicals will eventually be the most efficient medium of storing and manipulating information."[70] Most important, a DNA computer, like optical computers, can also carry out parallel functions simultaneously.

As promising as all these new types of computers are, they do present challenges. Engineers must first overcome problems of reliability, durability, and interconnectivity with other technologies before any of them become widely available. And if these exotic computer technologies are ever perfected, most likely their primary purpose would be to tackle large-scale operations such as code breaking. That means silicon-chip computers will most likely exist side by side with the new computer technologies and provide everyday services such as e-mail for many years. They may also co-exist with another type of computers: the hybrid. These crossbreed machines are the result of blending technologies based on both silicon and biologic systems.

A BLENDING OF TECHNOLOGIES

Computer chips may some day be imbedded into the human body and work in conjunction with living organisms. Some industry observers believe that within the next century physicians will be able to surgically implant computer chips into human beings to correct health problems such as those caused by disease and infirmity. In theory, at least, computer chips could even be placed in the human brain to facilitate learning. Scientists also expect a merging of human cells and computer chips to one day enable the deaf to hear, the blind to see, and the limbless to have synthetic arms and legs that function almost as well as natural ones.

Even more fantastic applications are predicted. High-tech futurists foresee the day when human beings receive tiny computerized sensor implants capable of temporarily intercepting the chemical-electrical signals from the five senses of the human body before they reach the brain. After these signals are blocked, the sensors would allow incoming signals from an outside source to reach the brain instead. The source of these alternate signals could be virtual reality software on a computer or even a website. Such mind-altering technology would enable individuals to experience inside their minds a new reality that far exceeds that provided by the 3-D computerized goggles and body-suits imbedded with sensors used in much of the virtual reality equipment today.

Meanwhile, other researchers are trying to create a different kind of reality—one that takes place in the "mind" of a machine. In short, they are trying to create machine intelligence.

WILL COMPUTERS THINK?

The quest to create machine, or artificial, intelligence (AI) dates back to World War II, when researchers began using computers to

Scientists strive to create machines with artificial intelligence that mimic the workings of the human brain as closely as possible.

decode secret messages. Today, AI research is underway in two main areas. One focuses on the building of new computer hardware needed to make AI work. The other seeks to understand how the human brain works, both psychologically and physically. AI researchers hope that insights gleaned from both these efforts will guide them in writing advanced computer software programs that emulate human thinking.

Some AI software is already used for tasks such as information processing, pattern recognition, and game playing. Various information-processing applications, for example, can scan written texts for grammar and syntax (word order) errors, and write summaries of longer passages. Some AI programs even recognize human speech and translate it into foreign languages.

AI is also being developed for diagnostic purposes. In medicine, for instance, computer programs can analyze symptoms, along with lab results and medical histories, to make diagnoses and prognoses. What makes this possible is an AI application known as an Expert System—software designed to make decisions as a real person would. The first step in designing such a system is to interview human experts to discover how they make decisions in their professions. Next, programmers transcribe this information into a computer program that uses a process called rule-based inference to enable computers to make decisions, diagnoses, or analyses as humans would.

Expert Systems, however, are still limited to whatever rules the software designer provides. Human thought, unlike current AI programs, also involves drawing on experience to solve problems.

Nonetheless, AI researchers are also making progress in developing this sort of intelligence as well. As Clive Davidson of *New Scientist* explains:

> A more recent approach has used neural networks—computer systems modelled loosely on the human brain. The programmer does not write a series of instructions for the network to carry out. Instead, the machine learns by trial and error to carry out the correct actions when given certain inputs. During the learning process, the properties of the network are gradually adjusted until a particular input produces the right output. This 'connectionist' approach has been successful in creating machines that can solve certain specific problems and has the advantage that the programmer does not have to specify exactly how a problem is to be solved.[71]

SMART TECHNOLOGY

Though machine consciousness may seem a remote possibility, more down-to-earth AI applications called smart technologies are in use right now. Using an array of AI high-tech sensors and microprocessors, these systems are able to detect patterns, images, motions, temperatures, and changes in pressure and then execute various commands. A smart missile, for example, has an onboard optical device that scans the earth below, compares the images with a digital map stored in the weapon's computerized memory, and adjusts the missile's trajectory.

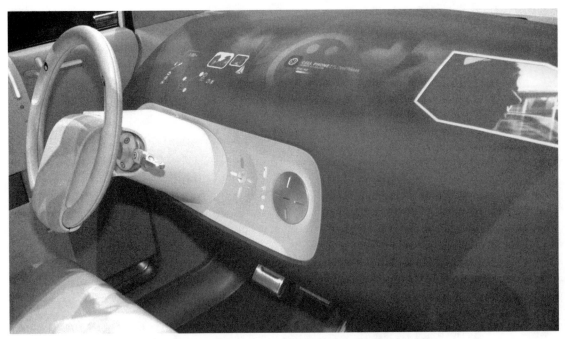

The driver of this pickup truck can customize the instrument panel on the dashboard by voice activation and receive weather reports and route assistance through the Internet.

Smart technology also has benign uses. Smart navigational systems are being introduced in some automobiles to help guide motorists through unfamiliar cities. A smart wheelchair developed at the University of Osaka in Japan in 1999 may soon prove to be a boon for the severely disabled. A video camera attached to the chair is focused on the passenger. When the passenger moves his or her face in a certain direction, the wheelchair moves forward. Certain head nods serve to propel or stop the wheelchair. And if the passenger is away from the chair, she or he can summon it with a hand gesture.

Smart technologies are also appearing in new homes and buildings around the world. Light switches and thermostats turn off automatically when heat sensors detect that no one is in the room. Other sensors notify the homeowner if a window or door is open. A security camera shows an image on the television or computer screen of the person at the door. All the functions can be controlled with a PC.

At present, scientists around the globe are also assembling various AI technologies in computerized robots. Though these machines may not yet be self-aware, they can still carry out many tasks that require intelligence. Once thought to be mere fantasies of science fiction writers, robots are taking over more work from humans. Some, for example, perform routine manufacturing tasks in factories, such as welding and assembling parts on automobiles.

Despite all these achievements in AI research, many observers are disappointed that the elusive goal of true intelligence is still far away. Some AI researchers doubt humans will ever make machines that can match or even surpass human thought. Others, however, remain optimistic and believe it is only a matter of time until highly advanced intelligent computerized systems exist across the world that are not limited to programming and will think independently.

And will computers ever be self-conscious? Ray Kurzweil, chairman and CEO of Kurzweil Technologies and author of *The Age of Spiritual Machines, When Computers Exceed Human Intelligence,* thinks with a little help from biology, they will be self-conscious. He predicts:

> Machines will claim to be conscious in 30 years. These claims will be largely accepted. Some philosophers will demur, saying that you cannot be conscious unless you're based on DNA-guided protein synthesis. But in my view, the idea of humans merging their own technology is just the next step in evolution, and represents a continuation of human-machine civilization. By 2099, there will be a strong trend toward a merger of human thinking with the world of machine intelligence.[72]

WILL COMPUTERS BECOME LIVING BEINGS?

If that day ever comes, human beings may face new and disturbing ethical questions. If a highly advanced AI system can ever think, as a biological being can think for itself and be self-conscious, would it also be alive?

And would such an intelligence be entitled to certain legal, moral, and civil rights?

Skeptics scoff at such speculations and point out that the essence of life is an ephemeral, mysterious, perhaps God-given force that no amount of technological tinkering could ever replicate. As they see it, all computers are merely machines, capable of operating only in a mechanistic, rule-based manner. Some critics even call upon AI researchers to give up their quest to create artificial intelligence and turn their energies instead to more conventional pursuits.

Undaunted, the champions of intelligent computer-based technology often respond by questioning the definition of the word "life" itself. They point out that many complex computer software systems now in

A PC user inspects a virus received via e-mail. Some analysts maintain that viruses may be considered an artificial life form.

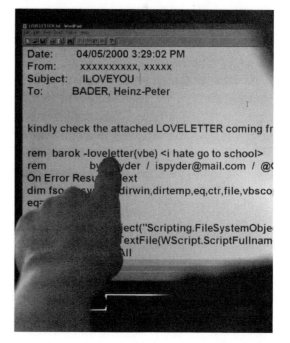

use already satisfy the most basic requirements of life—features that include growth, motion, and the ability to replicate themselves. Some thinkers believe computer viruses act as if they were alive. Explains *Newsweek* writer Adam Rogers, "In the most radical view, [computer] viruses are an artificial life form. They live, breed, evolve, procreate and die."[73]

Rodney Brooks, director of MIT's Artificial Intelligence Lab, thinks other computer programs are advanced enough to be close to meeting the definitions of life as well. He explains: "Computers programs that reproduce and evolve are starting to exhibit behaviors we expect from simple living creatures, such as interaction with complex environments and sexual reproduction. Artificial life forms that 'live' inside computers have evolved to the point where they can chase prey, evade predators and compete for limited resources."[74] Because of these startling ongoing developments, many leading scientists, philosophers, and computer engineers have gathered at international conferences in recent years to discuss the moral and ethical problems that might one day emerge if intelligent machines become thinking beings.

As researchers continue to develop AI systems, an even bigger life form may be evolving. In December 2000, Larry Smarr, a renowned astrophysicist, told the *New York Times* that the Internet, with its billions of computer connections, was becoming "the emerging planetary supercomputer."[75] In addition, Smarr had something even more startling to suggest about the increasingly complex Internet: "The real question from a software point of view is: Will it [the Inter-

net] become self aware?"[76] To Smarr, neither the question nor the answer is far-fetched. He believes it is possible that a huge intelligence emerging in cyberspace could evolve from the myriad billions of computer connections around the world.

Though not all computer engineers agree with Smarr, most would probably acknowledge that the Internet evolves every minute and that demand for access to it grows exponentially worldwide. To make it possible to handle the coming explosion of activity on the World Wide Web, however, the Internet must be dramatically upgraded. Plans to achieve that goal are already under way. Various universities and governmental bodies are now laying plans for building an Internet II.

PREPARING FOR THE FUTURE

As always, the past is the only guide for anticipating the future, and this is true of the Computer Revolution. In the late 1880s many Americans were awed by the new energy called electricity that flowed into their homes on copper wires. Since that time, electricity has transformed almost every aspect of human life on earth. Nobody alive in the late nineteenth century could have ever imagined that this strange new power would one day make possible inventions such as radio, television, VCRs, fax machines, the personal computer, and the Internet.

Many observers of the Computer Revolution expect its impact on the lives of human beings to be even more dramatic than what has already taken place. Some predict that the growing number of on-line communities

THE INTERNET OF THE FUTURE

Vinton Cerf, the coinventor of the Internet Protocol known as TCP/IP, offers this glimpse of the future in a passage from an article he wrote for Time *magazine.*

An Internet-enabled mobile phone displays a map.

What will the Internet be like 20 years from now?

Like the rest of the infrastructure, the Internet will eventually seem to disappear by becoming ubiquitous. Most access will probably be via high-speed, low-power radio links. Most handheld, fixed and mobile appliances will be Internet enabled. This trend is already discernible in the form of Internet-enabled cell phones and personal digital assistants. Like the servants of centuries past, our household helpers will chatter with one another and with the outside help.

At some point, the armada of devices we strap to our bodies like tools on Batman's belt will coalesce into a smaller number of multifunction devices. Equipped with radio links, a PDA [personal digital assistant] can serve as an appliance-control remote, a digital wallet, a cell phone, an identity badge, an e-mail station, a digital book , a pager and perhaps even a digital camera.

So many appliances, vehicles and buildings will be online by 2020 that it seems likely there will be more things on the Internet than people. Internet-enabled cars and airplanes are coming online, and smart houses are being built every day. Eventually, programmable devices will become so cheap that we will embed them in the cardboard boxes into which we put other things for storage or shipping. These passive "computers" will be activated as they pass sensors and will be able to both emit and absorb information. . . .

The Internet will undergo substantial alteration as optical technologies allow the transmission of many trillions of bits per second on each strand of the Internet's fiber-optic backbone network. The core of the network will remain optical, and the edges will use a mix of access technologies, ranging from radio and infrared to optical fiber and the old twisted-pair copper telephone lines. By then, the Internet will have been extended, by means of an interplanetary Internet backbone, to operate in outer space.

in cyberspace will one day replace many of the person-to-person relationships common to most people today. Bound by common interests, not proximity, the new cyber neighborhoods may one day represent almost every special interest group known to humanity. Though physically separated, members of these electronic vicinities may interact with one another by voice, data, video, and other computerized technologies to a degree now unimaginable. This could mean that in the not-so-distant future, on-line recreating, learning, working, shopping, obtaining medical treatment, and traveling to distant lands by means of virtual reality will be the stuff of everyday life. MIT's

Nicholas Negroponte thinks these ideas are not too far away:

> We will socialize in digital neighborhoods in which physical space will be irrelevant and time will play a different role. Twenty years from now, when you look out a window, what you see may be five thousand miles and six time zones away. When you watch an hour of television, it may have been delivered to your home in less than a second. Reading about Patagonia can include the sensory experience of going there. A book by William Buckley [an American conservative political writer] can be a conversation with him.[77]

Owners can use this easy chair's computer jacks and wireless keyboard to access e-mail and surf the Web through their television sets.

Others, however, who also attempt to glimpse into the future, are more pessimistic than Negroponte. They tend to doubt claims that computers will substantially improve the lives of human beings. To many of these skeptics, computers are just machines, and the Internet a system that is only as good or bad as the culture that created it. *New York Times* writer Paul Goldberger, in fact, thinks the much-vaunted cyberspace is no replacement for true person-to-person interaction. He writes: "We hear constantly about cyberspace as a place of connections made between all kinds of people who would not have come together before. Perhaps. But every one of them has connected by being alone, in front of a computer screen, and this is a poor excuse for what community has meant for most of history."[78]

Only time will tell how the Computer Revolution finally shapes the lives of human beings. Just as the pioneers of the modern computer discovered, no one can anticipate what new insight, chance remark, or accidental discovery will send the ongoing revolution lurching off in a new direction.

With their abacuses and primitive devices designed to keep track of the world around them, ancient human beings set in motion a quest for more powerful and complex machines that even now promise to eclipse human power forever. Those machines and the societies they will affect, however, still lie ahead.

Notes

Introduction: A Quiet Revolution

1. Stewart Brand, "Is Technology Moving Too Fast?" *Time*, June 19, 2000, p. 108.

Chapter 1: Origins of the Revolution

2. Quoted in Stan Augarten, *Bit by Bit: An Illustrated History of Computers*. New York: Ticknor & Fields, 1984, p. 3.

3. Quoted in *Computer Basics: Understanding Computers*, by the editors of Time Life Books, Alexandria, VA: Time Life Books, 1985, p. 11.

4. Scott McCartney, *ENIAC: The Triumphs and Tragedies of the World's First Computer*. New York: Walker and Company, 1999, p. 17.

5. McCartney, *ENIAC*, p. 19.

6. Howard Rheingold, *Tools for Thought: The History and Future of Mind-Expanding Technology*. Cambridge, MA: The MIT Press, 2000, p. 38.

7. Quoted in McCartney, *ENIAC*, p. 50.

8. McCartney, *ENIAC*, p. 51.

9. McCartney, *ENIAC*, p. 86.

10. Quoted in Matt Crenson, "A Golden Year in the Computer Age." Portland, *Oregonian*, February 15, 1996, p. a14.

11. McCartney, *ENIAC*, p. 102.

Chapter 2: The Rapid Rise of Modern Computing Power

12. Bill Gates, *The Road Ahead*. New York: Viking, 1995, p. 11.

13. Robert X. Cringely, "Triumph of the Nerds," www.PBS.org/nerds/transcript.html.

14. Quoted in Robert X. Cringely, "Nerds 2.01," www.PBS.org/nerds2.01/index.html.

15. Gates, *The Road Ahead*, p. 16.

16. Gates, *The Road Ahead*, p. 16.

17. Quoted in Cringely, "Nerds 2.01."

18. Quoted in Cringely, "Nerds 2.01."

19. Quoted in Cringely, "Nerds 2.01."

20. Quoted in Cringely, "Nerds 2.01."

21. Quoted in Cringely, "Nerds 2.01."

22. Gates, *The Road Ahead*, p. 47.

Chapter 3: The Third Wave: Linking the Computers of the World

23. Quoted in Edwin Diamond and Stephen Bates, "The Ancient History of the Internet," *American Heritage Magazine*, October 1995, p. 42.

24. Quoted in Cringely, "Nerds 2.01."

25. Quoted in Diamond and Bates, "The Ancient History of the Internet," p. 45.

26. Quoted in Anick Jesdanun, "The World Wide Web Turns 10," *Star Banner*, December 24, 2000, p. 6d.

27. Quoted in Christos J. P. Moschovitis, Hilary Poole, Tami Schuyler, and Theresa M. Senft, *History of the Internet: A Chronology, 1843 to the Present*. Santa Barbara, CA: ABC-CLIO, 1999, p. 163.

28. Quoted in Anick Jesdanun,"The World Wide Web Turns 10," p. 6d.

Chapter 4: A Changing Society

29. Quoted in Steven Levy, "TechnoMania," *Newsweek*, February 27, 1995, p. 26.

30. Levy, "TechnoMania," p. 27.

31. Esther Dyson, *Release 2.0: A Design for Living in the Digital Age*. New York: Broadway Books, 1997, p. 8.

32. Dyson, *Release 2.0*, p. 3.

33. Quoted in Hank Schlesinger, "Cerf on the Web," *Popular Science*, March 2000, p. 52.

34. Peter Drucker, "Beyond the Information Revolution," *The Atlantic Monthly*, October 1999, p. 52.

35. Gates, *The Road Ahead*, p. 16.

36. Nicholas Negroponte, *Being Digital*. New York: Alfred A. Knopf, 1995, p. 199.

37. Clifford Stoll, *High-Tech Heretic: Why Computers Don't Belong in the Classroom and Other Reflections by a Computer Contrarian*. New York: Doubleday, 1999, p. xiii.

38. Henry Louis Gates Jr., "Black and Unplugged," *Teacher Magazine*, March 2000, p. 46.

39. Frederick L. McKissack Jr., "Cyberghetto," *The Progressive*, June 1998, pp. 20–22.

40. Gregory J. E. Rawlins, *Moths to the Flame: The Seductions of Computer Technology*. Cambridge, MA: The MIT Press, 1996, p. 85.

Chapter 5: Challenges to Society

41. Robert X. Cringely, *Accidental Empires: How the Boys of Silicon Valley Make Their Millions, Battle Foreign Competition, and Still Can't Get a Date*. New York: HarperCollins, 1996, p. 350.

42. Quoted in D. Ian Hopper, "Government Not Hacking E-Security," *Star Banner*, April 6, 2000, p. 3A.

43. Rawlins, *Moths to the Flame*, p. 18.

44. Maryanne Murray Buechner, "Filter Out the Filth," *Time Digital*, April 27, 1998, p. 50.

45. Peter F. Eder, "Privacy on Parade," *The Futurist*, July–August 1994, pp. 39–40.

46. Quoted in Maryanne Murray Buechner, "FBI Alum James Kallstrom Unscrambles Code Debate," *Time Digital*, April 28, 1998, p. 25.

47. Simson Garfinkel, "Privacy and the New Technology," *The Nation*, February 28, 2000, p. 15.

48. Quoted in Buechner, "Filter Out the Filth," p. 22.

49. Quoted in Buechner, *Time Digital*, p. 21.

50. Gary Ruskin, "Schools Aren't Market Research Factories," *American Teacher*, April 2001, p. 4.

51. Levy, "TechnoMania," *Newsweek*, p. 29.

52. Quoted in Schlesinger, "Cerf on the Web," p. 53.

Chapter 6: The Dark Side of the Computer Revolution

53. Dyson, *Release 2.0*, p. 6.

54. Quoted in Laurie Asseo, "Court to Rule on Online Child Pornography," *Star Banner*, January 23, 2001, p. 3a.

55. Quoted in Suzanne Rico, "Police Struggle with Cyberstalking," December 17, 2000. http:abcnews.go.com/sections/tech/DailyNews/cyberstalking000501.html.

56. Quoted in Rico, "Police Struggle With Cyberstalking."

57. Quoted in Jack Smith, "FBI Responds to New Wave of Cybercrime," March 30, 2001. www.infowar.com/law/00/law_040700c_j.shtml.

58. Rawlins, *Moths to the Flame*, p. 118.

59. Rawlins, *Moths to the Flame*, p. 118.

60. Tom Peters, "What Will We Do for Work?", *Time*, May 22, 2000, p. 68.

61. Levy, "TechnoMania," p. 26.

62. Drucker, "Beyond the Information Revolution," p. 50.

63. Levy, "TechnoMania," p. 29.

64. Quoted in Norm Alster, "Are Old PCs Poisoning Us?", *Business Week*, June 12, 2000, p. 78.

65. Rawlins, *Moths to the Flame*, p. 97.

66. Quoted in Dave Grossman, *On Killing: The Psychological Cost of Learning to Kill in War and Society*. Boston: Little, Brown and Company, 1996, p. 169.

67. Grossman, *On Killing*, p. 170.

Chapter 7: An Unfolding Awesome Power

68. Negroponte, *Being Digital*, p. 6.

69. Quoted in Peter McGrath, "If All the World's a Computer," *Newsweek*, January 1, 2000, p. 72.

70. John S. MacNeil, "The Wet and Wild Future of Computers," *U.S. News & World Report*, February 14, 2000, p. 52.

71. Clive Davidson, "Robots: The Next Generation," *New Scientist*, January 14, 1995, www.newscientist.com/home.html.

72. Quoted in John R. Quain, "Will Computers Think on Their Own?", *Popular Science*, March 20, 2000, p. 55.

73. Adam Rogers, "Is There a Case for Viruses?", *Newsweek*, February 27, 1995, p. 65.

74. Rodney Brooks, "Will Robots Rise Up and Demand Their Rights?", *Time*, June 19, 2000, p. 86.

75. Quoted in John Markoff, "The Soul of the Ultimate Machine," December 10, 2000 www.NewYorkTimes.com.

76. Quoted in Markoff, "The Soul of the Ultimate Machine."

77. Negroponte, *Being Digital*, p. 7.

78. Quoted in Jane M. Healy, Ph.D., *Failure to Connect: How Computers Affect Our Children's Minds—for Better and Worse.* New York: Simon & Schuster, 1998, p. 195.

For Further Reading

Elizabeth Marshall, *A Student's Guide to the Internet: Exploring the World Wide Web, Gopher Space, Electronic Mail, and More.* Brookfield, CT: Millbrook, 1996. A concise and informative primer on how to understand and navigate the Internet.

Donald D. Spencer, *An Invitation to Computers.* Ormond Beach, FL: Camelot Publishing, 1989. Though dated, this book's section on computer history is informative and useful.

Donald D. Spencer, *The Timetable of Computers: A Chronology of the Most Important People and Events in the History of Computers.* Ormond Beach, FL: Camelot Publishing, 1999. A detailed reference book that outlines the rise of computers in a chronological, encyclopedic fashion.

Paul A. Winters, ed., *Computers and Society,* San Diego: Greenhaven Press, 1997. Part of the publisher's Current Controversies series, this volume includes many interesting articles on various contentious issues about the role of computers in human life.

Paul A. Winters, ed., *The Information Revolution.* San Diego: Greenhaven Press, 1998. An interesting compilation of essays on the impact of computer technology on society.

Works Consulted

Books

Stan Augarten, *Bit by Bit: An Illustrated History of Computers*. New York: Ticknor & Fields, 1984. A richly illustrated and readable history for both the scholar and the general reader.

Tim Berners-Lee with Mark Fischetti, *Weaving the Web: The Original Design and Ultimate Destiny of the World Wide Web*. New York: HarperSanFrancisco, 1999. A detailed account of the creation of the World Wide Web, coauthored by the man who invented it.

Martin Campbell-Kelly and William Aspray, *Computer: A History of the Information Machine*. New York: BasicBooks, 1996. An informative history of the invention of the computer for both scholars and general readers.

Computer Basics: Understanding Computers, by the editors of Time Life Books, Alexandria, VA: Time Life Books, 1985. A dated but well-written and illustrated collection of essays on various aspects of computers.

Robert X. Cringely, *Accidental Empires: How the Boys of Silicon Valley Make Their Millions, Battle Foreign Competition, and Still Can't Get a Date*. New York: HarperCollins, 1996. A witty and irreverent history of the personal computer.

Esther Dyson, *Release 2.0: A Design for Living in the Digital Age*. New York: Broadway Books, 1997. This lively book examines the impact of cyberspace on human society.

Thomas A. Easton, ed., *Taking Sides: Clashing Views on Controversial Issues in Science, Technology, and Society*. Guilford, CT: Dushkin/McGraw-Hill, 2000. A college-level collection of opposing essays on controversial issues related to technology.

Christopher Evans, *The Making of the Micro: A History of the Computer*. New York: VanNostrand Reinhold, 1981. Though dated, this well-written book covers the early days of the microcomputer.

Bill Gates, *The Road Ahead*. New York: Viking, 1995. A readable book about the computer revolution, written by one of the pioneers of the personal computer industry.

Dave Grossman, *On Killing: The Psychological Cost of Learning to Kill in War and Society*. Boston: Little, Brown and Company, 1996. A fascinating study for mature readers on the psychology of those who kill in wartime.

Jane M. Healy, Ph.D., *Failure to Connect: How Computers Affect Our Children's Minds—for Better and Worse*. New York: Simon & Schuster, 1998. A well-researched book with many examples of how computers help children learn, along with warnings about the dangers of overrelying on the new machines.

Scott McCartney, *ENIAC: The Triumphs and Tragedies of the World's First Computer*. New York: Walker And Company, 1999. A concise, well-written history.

Christos J. P. Moschovitis, Hilary Poole, Tami Schuyler, and Theresa M. Senft, *History of the Internet: A Chronology, 1843 to the Present*. Santa Barbara, CA: ABC-CLIO, 1999. A well-organized, readable history.

John Naisbitt with Nana Naisbitt and Douglas Phillips, *High Tech, High Touch: Technology and Our Search for Meaning*. New York: Broadway Books, 1999. A critique for the general reader of technology's impact on modern society.

Nicholas Negroponte, *Being Digital*. New York: Alfred A. Knopf, 1995. A lively examination of the ongoing digital revolution and its impact on computing and everyday life.

Gregory J. E. Rawlins, *Moths to the Flame: The Seductions of Computer Technology*. Cambridge, MA: The MIT Press, 1996. An interesting look at many of the social problems resulting from the Computer Revolution.

Howard Rheingold, *Tools for Thought: The History and Future of Mind-Expanding Technology*. Cambridge, MA: The MIT Press, 2000. An updated release of an earlier history of the computer.

David Ritchie, *The Computer Pioneers*. New York: Simon & Schuster, 1986. A lively account that explores the contributions and personalities of those involved in the development of modern computers prior to the rise of PCs. Technical explanations may be too detailed for some young readers.

Clifford Stoll, *High-Tech Heretic: Why Computers Don't Belong in the Classroom and Other Reflections by a Computer Contrarian*. New York: Doubleday, 1999. Written by a commentator, lecturer, and astronomer, this readable book takes a critical look at some of the claims made by computer advocates.

Paul Strathern, *Turing and the Computer*. New York: Anchor Books, Doubleday, 1997. A concise, interesting biography for the mature reader of computer pioneer Alan Turing.

Periodicals

Norm Alster, "Are Old PCs Poisoning Us?", *Business Week*, June 12, 2000.

Laurie Asseo, "Court to Rule on Online Pornography," Star Banner, January 23, 2001.

Stewart Brand, "Is Technology Moving Too Fast?", *Time*, June 19, 2000.

Rodney Brooks, "Will Robots Rise Up and Demand Their Rights?" *Time*, June 19, 2000.

Maryanne Murray Buechner, "Filter Out the Filth," *Time Digital*, April 27, 1998.

Maryanne Murray Buechner, "FBI Alum James Kallstrom Unscrambles Code Debate," *Time Digital*, April 28, 1998.

Vinton Cerf, "What Will Replace the Internet?", *Time*, June 19, 2000.

Jay Chiat, "How Will Advertisers Reach Us?", *Time*, May 22, 2000.

Matt Crenson, "A Golden Year in the Computer Age." Portland, *Oregonian*, February 15, 1996.

Edwin Diamond and Stephen Bates, "The Ancient History of the Internet," *American Heritage Magazine*, October 1995.

Peter Drucker, "Beyond the Information Revolution," *The Atlantic Monthly*, October 1999.

Peter F. Eder, "Privacy on Parade," *The Futurist*, July–August 1994.

Henry Louis Gates Jr., "Black and Unplugged," *Teacher Magazine*, March 2000.

Barry Golson and David Sheff, "The Geek Who Would Be President," *Yahoo Internet Life*, November, 2000.

Simson Garfinkel, "Privacy and the New Technology," *The Nation*, February 28, 2000.

D. Ian Hopper, "Government Not Hacking E-Security," *Star Banner*, April 6, 2000.

Anick Jesdanun, "The World Wide Web Turns 10," *Star Banner*, December 24, 2000.

Stephen King, "How I Got That Story," *Time*, December 18, 2000.

Steven Levy, "TechnoMania," *Newsweek*, February 27, 1995.

Steven Levy, "It's Time to Turn the Last Page," *Newsweek*, January 1, 2000.

John S. MacNeil, "The Wet and Wild Future of Computers," *U.S. News & World Report*, February 14, 2000.

Harry McCracken, "Garage Mechanics: The Apple Seedling," *PC World*, December 1999.

Aoife McEvoy, "Amazing Grace," *PC World*, December 1999.

Peter McGrath, "If All the World's a Computer," *Newsweek*, January 1, 2000.

Frederick L. McKissack Jr., "Cyberghetto," *The Progressive*, June 1998.

Chris O'Malley, "It's an Internet World," *Popular Science*, March 2000.

Tom Peters, "What Will We Do for Work?", *Time*, May 22, 2000.

John R. Quain, "Will Computers Think on Their Own?", *Popular Science*, March 20, 2000.

Adam Rogers, "Is There a Case for Viruses?", *Newsweek*, February 27, 1995.

Gary Ruskin, "Schools Aren't Market Research Factories," *American Teacher*, April 2001.

Hank Schlesinger, "Cerf on the Web," *Popular Science*, March 2000.

Clifford Stoll, "The Internet? Bah!", *Newsweek*, February 27, 1995.

Randall E. Stross, "A Gift for the Internet," *U.S. News & World Report*, December 18, 2000.

Nancy Zuckerbrod, "Government Web Sites May Violate Privacy," *Star Banner*, April 17, 2001.

Website

The California Academic and Vocational Information Exchange (www.Cavix.org/internet/history.htm). Cavix is a website sponsored by the Los Angeles County Office of Education on computing for educators.

Internet Sources

Andrew Chang and the Associated Press, "South Korean Deaths Linked to Internet Suicide Site," December 19, 2000. http://more.ABCNews.go.com/sections/world/DailyNews/suicide001219.html.

Robert X. Cringely, "Nerds 2.01," 1998. www.pbs.org/nerds2.01/index.html.

———, "Triumph of the Nerds," www.pbs.org/nerds/transcript.html.

Clive Davidson, "Robots: The Next Generation," *New Scientist*, January 14, 1995. www.newscientist.com/home.html.

Rich Hughes, "Cypherpunk's Manifesto," March 9, 1993. www.activism.net/cypherpunk/manifesto.html.

John Markoff, "The Soul of the Ultimate Machine," December 10, 2000. www.NewYorkTimes.com.

Suzanne Rico, "Police Struggle with Cyberstalking," December 17, 2000. http:abcnews.go.com/sections/tech/DailyNews/cyberstalking000501.html.

Jack Smith, "FBI Responds to New Wave of Cybercrime," March 30, 2001. www.infowar.com/law/00/law_040700c_j.shtml.

Bruce Sterling, "Short History of the Internet," *The Magazine of Fantasy and Science Fiction on Line*. Science Column 5, February 1993. www.lysator.liv/se/etexts./the_internet.htm.

Index

Picture Credits

About the Author

John M. Dunn is a freelance writer and high school history teacher. He has taught in Georgia, Florida, North Carolina, and Germany. As a writer and journalist, he has published more than three hundred articles and stories in more than twenty periodicals, as well as scripts for audio-visual productions and a children's play. His books, *The Russian Revolution, The Relocation of the North American Indian, The Spread of Islam, Advertising, The Civil Rights Movement, The Enlightenment, Life During the Black Death*, and *The Vietnam War: A History of U.S. Involvement* are published by Lucent Books. He lives with his wife and two daughters in Ocala, Florida.